ARCHAEOLOGY

INTERNATIONAL LIBRARY

SABATINO MOSCATI

ARCHAEOLOGY

COLLINS · PUBLISHERS   FRANKLIN WATTS, INC.

London · Glasgow   New York

CONTENTS

CHAPTER 1

WHAT IS ARCHAEOLOGY?

Not so many years ago, archaeology was considered a bore. People were largely indifferent to it. But nowadays it is a topical and popular science that anyone with a little curiosity can learn about. It is one of the achievements of modern writers on the subject that it now attracts interest far beyond a narrow circle of specialists. In fact, many of the archaeologist's triumphs (if not his techniques) have become part of the store of general knowledge. Furthermore, the latest archaeological finds "make news" along with politics, crime and sport in the columns of daily papers.

The famous French archaeologist André Parrot points out that some countries differed in their attitude to the subject. Early in 1934 he submitted an article about a discovery in Mari to the Editor of *L'Illustration*, only to be told without hesitation, "French people are not interested in archaeology!" Parrot goes on to say, "My article remained with the weekly magazine for eighteen months. Meanwhile the *Illustrated London News*, to whom I had submitted the same article following a friend's advice, published it, translated into English, a fortnight later, in an issue which was certainly not lacking in topical news since it reported the murder at Marseille on 31 October 1934 of King Alexander of Yugo-slavia and of Louis Barbhon, who had gone to meet him there. What is more the first page of the *Illustrated London News* did not carry a photograph of the murdered men, Parrot recalls, "but instead one of a statuette which I had discovered at Mari of the goddess Ishtar who, demure in her long and simple robe, was opening her eyes again after five thousand years of sleep."

But despite the recently awakened, wide interest, and although archaeology is now newsworthy, most people's knowledge of it does not go very deep. The gap between "producers" and "consumers" of this science has remained almost as wide as it ever was. The layman takes a great interest in discoveries, but he knows and understands very little of what goes on behind the scenes. This means that it is up to the expert to help him—especially since this interest, if it is not sustained by basic knowledge, may, and often does, lead to misunderstandings and misinterpretations. Rather than present discoveries as lucky or almost miraculous events, the expert should show how and why he has arrived at his conclusions, explaining each link in the chain of reasoning and research.

Efforts to inform the public should be regarded as a vital part of the archaeologist's activities. Complaints that the community mis-

Detail from a Middle Euphratean wall painting. (Louvre Museum, Paris)

A Roman magistrate and his wife on a fresco found in the ruins of Pompeii. (National Archaeological Museum, Naples)

understands or underestimates their needs (whether for money, equipment or facilities), should not be made before the scientists have done everything in their power to make themselves understood. And when they wax indignant about the lack of care with which the ruins of the past are treated, they must also ask themselves whether they have awakened and fostered an informed interest likely to encourage such care.

This kind of interest is essential if archaeology is to establish a public position comparable with that of other sciences. It can be done. The enormous number of British people who queued for hours to visit the Tutankhamun Exhibition in London proved without a doubt that interest in archaeology is no longer confined to a few, dusty academics and wealthy amateurs. The language of archaeology is less confusing to the layman than that of medicine or astronomy. Maintaining the public's interest is the only way to create an atmosphere in which the young can become interested in archaeology and develop this interest naturally. Archaeology is not taught in secondary schools, and even in universities there are not always as many courses as there should be; so the future of the subject depends almost entirely on the way it is presented to the community as a whole.

Definitions

The word "archaeology" comes from the Greek, and it means "the science of antiquity". We now use it to mean the study of the past through the artefacts, and any other tangible objects left behind, intentionally or otherwise, by past generations. This definition establishes that archaeology is particularly distinct from the study of documents—that is, from the written evidence left by ancient peoples. Such documents may be of interest to archaeologists (particularly in epigraphy, which is the study of inscriptions), but the literary, historical and cultural interpretation of the documents themselves is left to the experts in other sciences, such as philology, history and economics.

The nature of archaeological evidence is satisfyingly concrete: it generally comes to us much as it was left by its creators, or at least without being overlaid by the distortions and interpretations of later generations. A document is, without a doubt, more eloquent; but it is an indirect testimony, giving us opinions on things rather than showing the things themselves. An artefact, on the other hand, in the true sense includes every kind of material evidence; it is absolutely pure.

Archaeology is inseparable from objects, whether newly acquired through excavations or stored in museums and collections. In certain respects it resembles palaeography: the palaeographer deciphers texts that may then be interpreted by a literary expert; the archaeologist discovers objects that may influence a historian's interpretation of a whole age. But archaeologists are more than mere suppliers of material to the historians of culture and art: in fact archaeology is a well-defined technique geared to the service of interpretation and judgement, func-tions that an expert archaeologist cannot and does not wish to ignore. Indeed, because he is in possession of this technique he is the only person who is able to arrive at a complete evaluation of his material.

The "relic"

An object from the distant past possesses a particularly strong attraction—one which is inherent in every "relic". This term, when used to describe the bones of saints, conveys a feeling of reverence and awe that is equally appropriate to the evocative power of direct evidence. This is the essential charm of archaeology, as Masimo Pallotino, an Italian archaeologist has observed:

A gold coin showing the Emperor Constantius Chlorus being welcomed by the city of London. (Rheinisches Landesmuseum, Trier)

Tangible evidence strikes the imagination much more forcefully than memory and tradition, which need an intellectual effort. The attraction of archaeology lies in being able to cross the threshold over which the contemporaries of Socrates or Caesar passed innumerable times, in holding a goblet which actually touched their lips, in seeing their images in relief or in a painting just as they were seen by the unknown ancient craftsman who depicted them. Looking at these stones and objects, one has the impression of mysterious forces emerging, so powerful in their effect that they are able to conquer the span of countless centuries.

This explains why ordinary people become enthusiastic about discoveries which are linked to some famous person, place or event, whether historical or legendary. Indeed, interest is at its most intense where legends are involved, because the evidence fits into the grand simplicities of the story-book and seems to confirm that a tale which has

worked upon the imagination—becoming more real than the facts of history—is actually part of history. Hence the clamour aroused by the so-called "discoveries" of Atlantis and of Noah's Ark, and the interest awakened in a vast public by the discovery near Lavino, at the beginning of 1972, of the place sacred to Aeneas' memory.

But if the emotive power of the "relic" is one of the major attractions of archaeology, it can also lead to misplaced enthusiasm (as in the cases of "Atlantis" and "Noah's Ark"). The confirmation of ancient traditions is not at all certain, and is not the primary function of archaeology. Like any other scientist, the archaeologist is not trying to confirm or deny anything, but rather to accumulate evidence. Using books like the Bible and the works of Homer as documentary sources is normally foreign to the methods and spirit of archaeology, and can be dangerous because the

Opposite: the gate of the Tripylon at Persepolis.

Far right: head of a king, reputably Hammurabi. Right: Marcus Aurelius. (Louvre Museum, Paris)

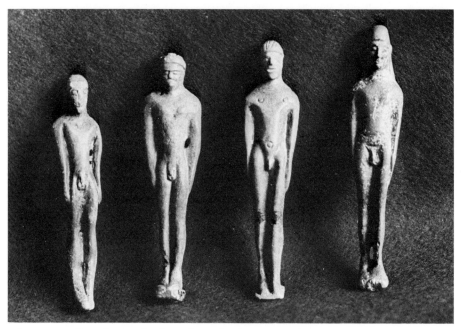

Bronze statuettes from the altar area at Lavino.

relevance of such works is cultural or literary.

But clues can be found and the careful use of ancient documents can fill in the background to archaeological finds, while scientific results can help to interpret historical manuscripts. One archaeologist who did use the works of Homer to great effect was the German, Heinrich Schliemann who used the *Iliad* when excavating Troy.

The buried museum

There is another point to be considered in comparing documents and objects recovered by the archaeologist. Generally, the literary inheritance of antiquity is known, for it has been handed down through the ages by various means. Great discoveries are still made, such as the papyri of Oxyrhynchus in Greek literature and the Dead Sea Scrolls,

Two heads from Lavino. The one on the right shows the influence of Greece on the style of the period, while that on the left reflects the stylization of the age.

which threw so much light on religious fervour in Jesus' time. Such new and significant acquisitions are always possible, but are very rare. This explains why philologists concentrate on interpreting rather than searching for documents.

In archaeology the situation is very different. In countries such as Greece and Italy, where very ancient cultures have been established, there is an impressive heritage of consolidated knowledge. But in these very countries there have been discoveries in recent times that have transformed our knowledge of antiquity. The Mycenaean finds at Santorin and in other parts of Greece, the paintings at Paestum, the stelae of Gargano and those at Mozia in Italy, are all cases in point. In these and later discoveries a new technique of research is being used that is described later in this book.

New knowledge comes to light all the time as archaeological methods are gradually applied to countries hitherto scarcely explored. Techniques that proved their value in Mesopotamian desert wastes are now used in the deserts of central Asia, and work of the sort carried out on the Iranian and Afghan plateaux has been extended to those of South America. In these places marvellous remains are produced

A colourful mask discovered at Mycenae. (National Museum, Athens)

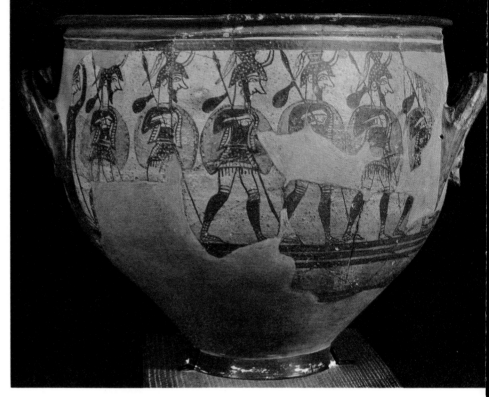

Warriors of the Mycenean Age decorate this Greek bowl, known as a krater. (National Museum, Athens)

Two examples of early tomb painting. (Superintendent of Antiquities of the Provinces of Salerno, Avellino and Benevento.)

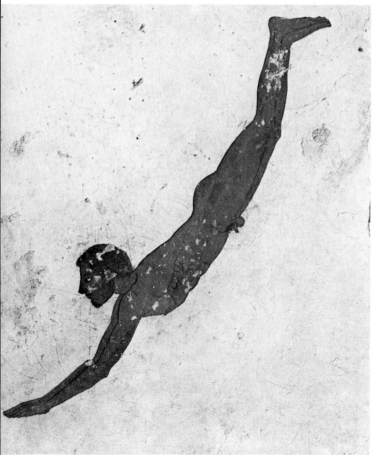

from practically nothing, revealing flourishing and advanced cultures where one might have expected only a few crude tools. Though the brief existence of high cultures was known in these countries, they now appear as part of a lengthy historical and cultural development.

It has been said that under our feet there is a buried "museum",

Three examples of stelae *decoration*. Stelae are upright blocks of stone, carved with figures or inscriptions, widely used in prehistoric times. They are of great importance in dating a site.

of which the part already located is very small compared with that which is still unknown. The objection could be raised that as the "museum" is buried, we cannot be sure it exists. The obvious answer is that where parts of artefacts and cities are unearthed, the earth must conceal other parts. This is now quite certain even where excavations have not yet started, because modern instruments and techniques such as aerial photography, analysis of the electrical resistance of the earth, and the analysis of magnetism, make possible an "X-ray" that reveals the buried objects.

Unlike many other researchers, therefore, archaeologists can often be certain that their efforts will be rewarded by success—so much so that sometimes it is decided not to dig until adequate publicity has been ensured and all means have been organized to bring the excavation to completion (which is not always easy). To excavate or not to excavate? This question is frequently

These excellent examples of stelae carving have survived for thousands of years.

One of the fabulous bull-men that guard the palace of Xerxes I at Persepolis in Iran.

debated among archaeologists, even when confronted by positive evidence; it is a sure sign of the wealth of possibilities which their discipline offers.

Travel through time

Archaeology is a great adventure, endowed with all the attractions of research into, and discovery of, the unknown. It is all the more fascinating since this research (and the discovery that may follow it) can be carried out in two usually irreconcilable dimensions: time and space. The common denominator of these two very different dimensions lies in the fact that they are distanced from us for chronological or geographical reasons.

Of the two dimensions, the chronological is without doubt the more important. Archaeology has traditionally been concerned with prehistory and the ancient world, and its more recent application to medieval and later times does not change its fundamental concern with

the past. Travel through the ages is, therefore, the attraction—but why? We have already mentioned the attraction of the "relic"; and in addition there is the intellectual prize that may be summarized in the phrase "knowledge by comparison". We cannot understand fully our own time unless we compare it with past times, and realize just how much we take for granted that other cultures have done without or even rejected. Such intellectual conquest is often more difficult and slower than might be supposed.

Let us take a few examples. Some are likely to make us feel that the human race has made progress over the centuries. When we look at Mesopotamian art, anonymous and often standardized, we come to understand that individual feeling and expression belong to later ages of artistic creation. When we think of the hundreds of children sacrificed by the Carthaginians to their gods, we come to understand that progress *has* been made by religion and that respect for the individual is a

A remarkably well-preserved fresco from the tomb on the Via Portuenese in Rome. By studying the detail, archaeologists can learn a great deal about life in Ancient Rome. (National Museum, Rome)

A statue, carved out of hard diotrite, of Gudea who ruled Lagash in Mesopotamia. (Louvre Museum, Paris)

quite recent development in historical terms. We have to tackle the difficulties of ancient writings, and to survey their spasmodic occurrence and survival, to realize the profound transformation that has taken place in the way we communicate and record events for posterity.

All the same, it would be wrong to give the impression that there has been an unvarying evolutionary progress taking place over a succession of civilizations. There can be no doubt that technology has advanced, but it is by no means certain that we have progressed morally and intellectually. Throughout the world innocent victims are still "sacrificed" as a result of ideological strife. Such progress as there has been is subject to sharp setbacks. Therefore the attraction of travel through time is not a moralistic

The mask of Quetzalcoatl, sacred to the Maya civilization of Mexico. (British Museum, London).

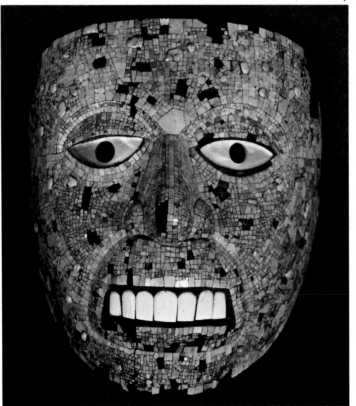

one, but it is a way of gaining knowledge, and it is not possible to gain knowledge without making comparisons. Without doubt, archaeology is a major source of concrete evidence for such comparisons.

Travel through space

Adventure in space is another lure of archaeology. An archaeologist usually has to travel, sometimes a short distance, sometimes thousands of miles. A supervisor in charge of the excavation of a specified area may reside in the biggest city in that area. Again and again his telephone will ring to announce sudden discoveries in near-by cities or in the open countryside. The increase in public works of all kinds (and, in particular, of road-building) has led to periodic and unexpected discoveries of buried monuments and settlements. It then becomes necessary to make haste, to ascertain the authenticity of the remains, and to arrange for the protection of the finds even before starting excavation. Although he has a home and an office, the archaeologist must always be ready to move, and to move quickly.

This is even more obvious in the case of the site-excavators, who are often stationed in remote regions and remain there during the whole period of the work. Exposed to all kinds of weather, in abnormal surroundings and sometimes enduring primitive living conditions, the excavator is usually a quiet scholar who would certainly never normally spend long periods in the open countryside, among forests, or on deserted beaches. Yet more and more he is called away to distant, unknown lands—not as a tourist but for hard work and an important and satisfying personal and professional experience.

This expansion of archaeology in space is one of the typical features of the modern discipline. Up to a few decades ago, classical culture dominated our view of the past to such an extent that the greater part of research at any given time was concentrated on it. The result was that Italy and Greece were the "native lands"—homes from home —of archaeologists. And when archaeologists did go to any other country, it was usually to look for traces of Greek or Roman colonization or influence.

Today the situation is totally different. The achievements of non-European cultures (for example in Africa and Oceania) have been revalued, and as a result archaeology has taken on other dimensions. The drastic reduction of travelling times through modern means of transport, especially the aeroplane, has hastened this trend. Nowadays many important excavations are in progress all over the world, and the archaeologist has become a traveller of a special kind, not limited by tourist conventions and fortunate enough to experience long and fruitful contacts with worlds utterly different from his own. The outcome of all this is the end of the mistaken sense of superiority that Europeans once displayed, and the achievement of a more universal and positive outlook.

The "detectives" of the past

A few years ago, a German journalist known by the assumed name of C. W. Ceram achieved great success with a book called *Gods, Graves and Scholars*, which describes the great archaeological discoveries made in the past. The secret of this success may be summarized in the subtitle "The Story of

The remains at Camiro. Years of painstaking excavation unearthed these magnificent remains. Even the layman can appreciate the satisfaction that the "dig" must have felt when they finished their work.

Archaeology", emphasizing the element of narrative adventure. Ceram actually uses the word "Roman", which is German and French for "novel".

"Even the most complicated scientific problems"—writes Ceram—"may be presented clearly and pleasantly if they are illustrated in the process of their development; if, that is to say, the reader is led along the same path already covered by the scientist from the moment of his inspiration to the final result." This explains "the eager interest that is awakened in the public—because of its dynamic drama—the deviations, the cross-roads, the blind alleys by which the archaeologist is, for various reasons, so attracted, such as human inadequacy, lack of thought, upsetting accidents, and external influences."

Archaeological "events", then, make up a sort of novel, pivoted on human adventures. The same might be said of various other sciences, though it seems to have a special appropriateness to archaeology because the subject so closely resembles police work or judicial inquiries. Journalists often refer to "detective work" by archaeologists, and it is doubtless significant that Agatha Christie, the famous writer of detective novels, has made obvious use of the diggings in which she took part with her archaeologist husband Sir Max Mallowan, who has directed many excavations in the Middle East and who has written a number of books on his work.

Let us take a closer look at the archaeologist's activities. Confronted with the few and dissimilar objects belonging to the past, he

A typical sarcophagus of Ptolemic Egypt.

Collecting and "treasure-hunting"

Most archaeologists strongly believe that the most important source of interest in archaeology is, without a doubt, the objects still waiting to be unearthed. Occasionally the tangible evidence of the past takes the form of jewels and treasures placed in tombs with the dead. The "Atreus treasure" at Mycenae and the tomb of Tutankhamun in the Egyptian Valley of the Kings show that such finds are really possible. To collectors and thieves, the search for treasure is generally the strongest attraction of archaeology; but even the professional archaeologist is not always indifferent to the lure of treasure and it is certainly difficult to blame him, when one considers the temptations which may come his way.

People who search for treasure may wish to profit by it, preserve it, adorn themselves and their property with it, or they may be possessed by the passion we call "collecting". It is ironic to observe that some model citizens, who would be very indignant if they saw anybody walking on a flower-bed, see nothing wrong in keeping illegally obtained archaeological objects in their homes, and indeed show them off in handsome heavily carved display-cabinets or in specially lit corners of their drawing rooms.

Treasure-hunting and collecting are thus two of the most powerful reasons why people become interested in archaeology. But, as we have seen, they are all too often accompanied by unworthy motives. Treasure-hunting is only a small part of archaeology, though a beneficial one in that it provokes sensational interest.

Excavations, however, must be organized with a very different end in mind, to reconstruct the past

One of the treasures of Mycenae discovered by Schliemann. He believed it to be the mask of Agamemnon, greatest of the Mycenaean kings, but it was later established as the funerary mask of a much earlier ruler.

must find out to whom they belonged and with which event they are connected. He must sift the evidence for proof that will enable him to reconstruct events; each item must be evaluated by comparison with others and "placed" in relation to them like pieces from a scattered mosaic, for only a sufficient number of accurately placed pieces will reveal the general pattern. The analysis, insight, effort and speculative thought exercised in the archaeologist's feats of reconstruction place him on a similar footing to the detective and the lawyer. And it has been observed that people who are interested in archaeology are often equally fond of reading detective novels and accounts of sensational trials, no doubt because they find the same intellectual satisfaction that they find in archaeology.

—not to destroy the evidence, but to store and evaluate it according to a coherent plan of research.

On the other hand, the archaeologist can turn to advantage the popular enthusiasm for detective work and treasure-hunting. In some countries patronage is necessary to finance and set up archaeological expeditions, but the patron may expect to be rewarded for his largesse with "treasures" from the site. One archaeologist who unearthed a Roman amphitheatre found himself in just such a situation and finally resolved the difficulty by extending his researches to a necropolis adjacent to his existing excavations which was much less significant for the reconstruction of the past but rich in objects left in the tombs, which were supplied to his patron and pacified his greed.

The most famous sarcophagus of them all—Tutankhamun's. (Museum of Antiquities, Cairo)

A statue of the Pharaoh Mentuhotep. (Museum of Antiquities, Cairo)

The Acropolis in Athens. Perhaps the most famous of all the glories of ancient Greece, the Acropolis has suffered from atmospheric pollution more in the last 25 years than throughout the 2,000 years of its existence.

Humanism and science

One respect in which archaeology is unique among modern sciences is the way in which it combines humanism with technology and science. The objective behind the reconstruction of ancient cultures, springs from the great tradition of Western humanism. But the means used to obtain the objective, from the pick and shovel to the more refined modern instruments of excavation and analysis, have a technical side which is recognized by everyone.

Today the term "subsidiary science" is frequently used by many archaeologists to describe chemistry, physics and botany in their roles as adjuncts to the discovery and study of ancient remains. Later, we look more closely at the part that these sciences play in locating remains and in evaluating and classifying them. The fact that the archaeologist of traditional training forwards discovered objects to a laboratory for scientific analysis should not deceive us: the workers in these laboratories are no longer outsiders but specialists working within the discipline of archaeology.

Archaeology in fact provides an example of the meeting between the humanities and the sciences which is one of the fundamental tendencies of the present time. The proficient archaeologist will experience the central insights of both and in doing so can be regarded as an example of the scientific humanism that ought to influence (as an aim if not as a realization) the course of the twentieth century.

Archaeology and tourism

People with a different training sometimes observe that a remarkable serenity and harmony exist in the world of archaeology. It is dangerous to generalize but it seems a fact that the heated arguments and controversies that afflict other sciences are rarely found here. Is it possible that this state of affairs owes something to life in the open air, to travel, and to the variety and richness of human experience that archaeology offers? Such factors are hard to assess, but the hypothesis seems worth considering.

If nothing else, archaeology is good for the health. Scientists, such as physicists and chemists, even when not confined to the laboratory, usually work indoors. The archaeologist needs to study books, but when he is on an excavation site he enjoys plenty of sun and light. As a result, he often comes into direct contact with the tourist; for tourists are visiting excavations in ever-increasing numbers, drawn by the fascination of "relics" of the past, and by the will-o'-the-wisp of treasure. And since ancient cultures usually flourished on places favoured by nature, cultural interest coincides with panoramic and climatic appeal. Archaeology has thus become connected with one of the liveliest of modern industries, producing the strange juxtaposition of ancient settlements and modern globe-trotters.

So much for motivations. People who are attracted by an activity want to practise it, so we must now find out how to go about it.

The Palatine in Rome. This is one of the major tourist attractions in Rome —believed to be the cradle of Roman civilization.

CHAPTER 2

TRAINING

People become archaeologists because they have a sense of vocation. It could be argued that all professions are chosen for this reason, but it is not true. Some people, for example, become doctors or lawyers because they want to follow in their parents' footsteps. Now, it is quite possible that a child may inherit a vocation for archaeology from his father or mother, but it must truly be a vocation, since he will certainly not inherit a "flourishing practice" or a number of clients. In other words he must start his career from scratch, and it is certainly not an easy one.

Some may choose their professions because they have been stimulated by an impressive example. If young people see a skilful engineer, lawyer or teacher at work, they may

The head of a female, carved in stone. This is typical of stone-carving from the Middle Euphrates. (Louvre Museum, Paris)

Gurnia—a Minoan village in north-eastern Crete.

be attracted, or at least influenced, by him, and may in time choose the same profession. But in archaeology the influence of example is much weaker: the number of people who can observe an archaeologist at work is very small and, therefore, the stimulus that comes from such an example is very much smaller than in other professions.

Furthermore for other studies, primary and secondary schools provide initial data which can later be developed at university. The chemist, the physicist and the biologist study their subjects from an early age and, having been compelled to do so, have been able to discover that they interest them. Once an interest has been developed in a subject pupils can drop the subjects that will be of little use to them and concentrate on those which will help gain an entry to University. Archaeology, on the other hand, is taught only at university level, and even there it is only one aspect of historical study. In order to make it the subject of specialization and then of a profession, it requires a particularly strong and accurately focused interest.

The existence of this sense of vocation is confirmed by the growing number of unprofessional enthusiasts in every country. Such people have never had the stimulus of university training, but in spite of this devote a remarkable amount of energy and effort to archaeology. They come from every walk of life. Many live far from cultural and scholarly centres yet retain a passionate devotion to archaeology. It would be wrong to dismiss them: we must remember that such enthusiasts made some of the most important discoveries of all time. We shall return to them later, after considering the professional archaeologist.

The professional man

A professional archaeologist has had a regular training and practises archaeology as a career, though not a very profitable one. Archaeologists generally are not very wealthy (unless they have incomes from other sources); in all countries the archaeologist's income is enough to earn a modest living and no more. This aspect of the profession should add to our respect for the work accomplished in it. Nor is this work without risks: the archaeologist may be forced to work in difficult or even dangerous terrain, and often has to contend with complex legal difficulties that arise over the ownership of finds. One certainly needs a sense of vocation!

But how does a person with this vocation train for such a profession? Although conditions vary from country to country, university is the place to study archaeology. It may be taught as one or more disciplines, along with Classical and Oriental archaeology, topography, epigraphy, numismatics and so on, converging towards the training of the archaeologist. One point is nevertheless clear: theory is not enough. It is no substitute for practical experience on the excavation site, and to this need each country provides its own answer.

The best universities usually have their own excavation quarters, either at home or abroad. Advanced students are sent to these quarters, where they can gain the necessary skills under expert supervision. Sometimes there are model quarters —that is, excavations which take place on sites particularly favourable for learning. In any case, excavation on site is necessary, for students pursuing this course, from the very start of their university

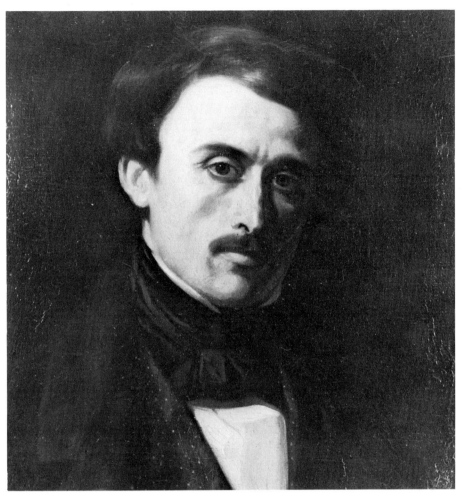

careers. Purely theoretical courses are only for those who require a less deep acquaintance with the subject, usually as part of some other course of study.

Another necessary element in an archaeologist's training is museum knowledge. This, first of all, because museums provide direct illustrations of what is taught, and more generally because they offer quantities of material for study and research. The student should bear in mind that the publicity given to archaeological material is not, on the whole, very satisfactory. Especially in countries rich in archaeological remains, there is a vast amount of material kept in dusty show-cases or stored in cellars that is almost unknown. Hence the jocular expression in archaeological circles, "excavations in museums": anyone who is interested may find, in show-cases or in store, unpublished material which is found to be of outstanding importance.

Having said all this, it must be admitted that a certain dualism exists between field and indoor archaeologists in some countries. This is particularly true of countries such as Italy, in which archaeological objectives are divided between the universities (which are responsible for teaching) and other bodies responsible for the preservation of material. It may happen that the professor will take on the role of an art historian while one

The donjon of the acropolis at Mount Sirai.

of his staff assumes that of the archaeologist: the name "Archaeology and History of Art". given to many Italian university chairs, reflects this situation.

The specialist

As well as learning the general techniques of archaeological research the student must familiarize himself with applied history, linguistics, the study of race and other specialist subjects. Courses in these subjects are normally only offered in universities, although there are a few institutes in various countries which have facilities for such studies.

One of these worthy of mention is the German Archaeological Institute, which has bases in most

countries where there are possibilities of archaeological research. They are well equipped with libraries and laboratories. Young scholars are allowed to spend periods of training and research, usually on the spot at suitable excavation sites. A roughly similar state of affairs prevails in French, English and American colleges, which make it possible for their students to work in various other countries where there are excavation sites. Each country has tended to become associated with some specific area of archaeological study, and there is no doubt that, as in other disciplines, the future will bring increasingly specialized training.

In our time we are seeing the progressive emergence of the Etruscologist, Orientalist, Americanist

and many other specialists in a given culture, while the various types of work and materials to be studied have produced a different kind of specialist in the epigraphist, the numismatist, the topographer, the anthropologist, and so on. There is as yet no sign of an end to the progressive widening of horizons that has characterized the development of modern archaeology.

The amateur

Everything that has been said so far is valid for the professional man. What about the amateur? What can we do about the potential contribution of the untrained enthusiast? Reject it? Harness it? Condition it? First of all we must acknowledge the contribution that amateurs have made in the past. Schliemann who discovered the ruins of Troy and the treasures of Mycenae, Belzoni who excavated the temples of Abu Simbel and entered the Pyramid of Giza, Botta who unearthed Nineveh, Dennis who discovered the Etruscan cities—these are just a few examples that indicate how much archaeology owes to amateurs in all countries throughout the ages.

"Well, that was a long time ago,"

a professional might say, remembering with horror the methods adopted during nineteenth-century excavations and reflecting that even today amateurs are a cause of problems and worries. Hurried, over-enthusiastic, sloppy excavations damage materials, and objects removed or kept hidden for fear of losing them may never be recovered. All this complicates the already difficult lives of qualified archaeologists, and one possible response is to ignore completely amateurs and refuse them facilities on the grounds of inadequate training.

This attitude is not really satisfactory. No problem is solved by denying its existence and refusing to think about it. That is why there are some archaeologists who take a more moderate attitude, maintaining that the contribution of the amateur, if properly organized and controlled, can be a help rather than a hindrance. The latest development in this field took place in Italy, a country particularly involved in the problem because of the richness of its ancient remains. Under the patronage of some professional archaeologists, the Archaeoclub was formed, open to anyone—pro-

A Ninevehan fragment showing a Assyrian archer.

fessional or amateur—with a strong interest in the subject and the time to spare.

What kind of tasks are given to this "extra reserve of assistance"? First of all, members of the Archaeoclub can inform the professional archaeologist of anything that might be of interest and which might not yet be known to him. For example, if an ancient monument is discovered in some remote place, the club members will advise the nearest centre. Should a site or monument fall into decay through natural deterioration or because of vandalism, that too is reported. In other words, a valuable contribution can be made to "official" archaeology by civic conscience operating with free initiative and aimed at the protection and proper upkeep of the common heritage.

Furthermore, the club may issue a monthly bulletin and publish

A painted vase from Guatemala. (British Museum, London)

Giovanni Battista Belzoni (1778–1823), the Italian explorer and archaeologist who first opened the Tomb of Abu Simbel in 1817.

pamphlets; in other words, do everything in the way of informing public opinion that the professional archaeologist has neither the time nor the inclination to do. Contact with public opinion is established in a more vivid and immediate way than through professional journals, but more authentically than via newspapers. Among other things, this makes it possible to initiate campaigns in favour of raising subscriptions for excavations or restoration of damaged monuments, creating and rallying an informed public opinion.

The key question remains the desirability of amateurs participating in the excavations, since this is inevitably the focus of their enthusiasm. Complete participation by the amateur would obviously be undesirable, but so would absolute exclusion. After some basic training, volunteers can put themselves at the disposal of the professional for work requiring assistance under supervision. The amateur should be welcomed provided he is aware of his limitations, is adequately trained, and observes the necessary discipline. Archaeology must not become too exclusive. Given certain limitations and conditions, anyone should have an opportunity to play an active and valid part in it.

The pyramids of Mycerinus, Chephren and Cheops on the Giza plateau. Cheops' pyramid is usually referred to as the Great Pyramid.

CHAPTER 3

DISCOVERY

The remains of ancient civilizations are buried. The first question asked of archaeologists is often: why? Men are not moles; they do not live underground—why, then, are the remains buried underground?

There are several answers, beginning with natural causes. Let us imagine a desert, where the wind drives the sand along: an abandoned city will inevitably be covered up, and nobody will clear away the sand until the archaeologist arrives. Now let us imagine a coastline of which parts are flooded; the inhabitants are buried and disappear from sight. Finally let us picture a cave; its roof collapses, everything inside it is buried, its entrance is blocked, and all traces of it disappear for centuries or thousands of years.

More important than the natural causes is the human factor. The ways in which remains accumulate are frequently discussed in archaeological manuals. When buildings are being altered, parts are knocked down and paved areas are torn up. All unusable materials are buried to provide the new buildings with more solid foundations, so the new houses are built on a higher level. Later, fires or wars may destroy the city and more remains will accumulate. The resulting debris will be too bulky to remove and will simply be hammered down and levelled off to make a new horizontal base. That is why the foundations of ancient cities always consist of several layers, representing progressively older phases of the city's past the deeper archaeologists dig.

These areas are the objects of the archaeologist's investigation. But how does he know where to look? There are no "discoverer's do-it-yourself handbooks". Nevertheless, looking back on past discoveries, we find constant features which help to locate the remains of buried cities. We must add that these features are not always apparent and not always present, and that pure luck as well as a systematic and organized research plays a part in the archaeologist's work.

A question of luck

The Italian writer and diplomat Macchiavelli claimed that luck played a 50 per cent part in all human affairs. This seems a reasonable figure to assign to the archaeologist's activities, though always taking into account his particular circumstances. For luck does not strike anywhere and anyhow; in fact we can very often single out phenomena which favour its operation.

Some discoveries seem almost miraculous. "Daddy, look at these painted bulls!" a little Spanish girl suddenly shouted. She and her

The synagogue at Ostia. The columns of the tabernacle have been restored to what they were when the building was a place of worship.

The corbels of the synagogue at Ostia are decorated with the traditional Jewish candelabra.

father were walking along in a dark cave at Altamira about a hundred years ago; and she had spotted one of the most extraordinary series of prehistoric paintings in Europe.

One of the most dramatic of all accidental discoveries was made in quite recent times by a Bedouin shepherd boy. One of his goats strayed, and to follow it the boy had to climb one of the cliffs rising above the shores of the Dead Sea. As boys will, he threw a stone into the cave—and heard something break. When, later on, he plucked up the courage to return with a friend, the boys found a number of earthenware jars. Inside were long rolls of dried-up manuscript in a strange language—manuscript that eventually reached, and shook, the learned world. These were the now-famous Dead Sea Scrolls, written by members of the Hebrew Essene sect in Palestine, and providing major new evidence about religious life in the time of Jesus.

In other cases there is a higher probability of discoveries being made. There are people whose job is to dig, for example the farmers who plough the fields and labourers on building sites and roadworks. All these people can be of great help to archaeologists, though they can also be dangerous if not warned or stopped in time. The Jewish Synagogue at Ostia was discovered while a new road was being made, fortifications and quays of the Greek port were unearthed in the Marseille Stock Exchange district during the urban reorganization of the town, and the construction of Heathrow Airport in London revealed a Celtic temple belonging to the First Iron Age.

Occasionally, remains of vanished cultures emerge suddenly as a result of natural phenomena, such as the effects of water and winds. At the little English town of Cromer, tidal erosion uncovered huge flint flakes and other materials. At Zürich an exceptional drought drained the waters of the lake, revealing a prehistoric palafitte, of which nothing was known before. Alongside these natural phenomena there are the forms of destruction caused by wars, which unfortunately aid the archaeologists. During the Second World War for example large areas of Cologne and London were laid bare, and became excavation zones as a result of bombings.

Archaeological remains on the surface

Many remains of archaeological interest are still visible. Famous examples are the Greek temples at Paestum and Selinunte, which have continued to stand over the centuries (although in a more or less ruinous state, because they happen to be in under-developed regions in which there was no incentive to build over them) and the Pantheon in Rome, erected during the Emperor Augustus' reign, restored by Hadrian, and later converted into a church. Such monuments may have others next to or underneath them; the ruined Temple of Antas, in Sardinia, revealed, while restorations were in course, an earlier Carthaginian building containing ornate votive objects.

In a more subtle way, even the layouts of cities are archaeological facts. Naples, Cologne and Vienna have all, surprisingly, retained the layout they had in Greek and Roman times, and therefore the streets, buildings and harbours of antiquity can be traced from their modern counterparts. Continuity of function is another possible indication of the presence of remains:

The Temple of Neptune at Paestum, in Italy. For 300 years, up to 400 B.C., there was a Greek colony here known as Poseidonia.

thus excavations of churches often reveal older churches and, earlier still, buildings used for pagan cults.

Information drawn from the appearance of the surface may be indirect, but none the less effective. In some regions, remains of ancient cities are clearly visible because the earth or sand has formed a compact covering around them, in the shape of flat-topped hillocks: thus in the Near East it is easy to distinguish natural mounds from the artificial ones that cover buried cities. Let us now look at another example, a field of grass under which there are ancient walls. During an arid summer the grass will dry more rapidly in places where the layer of earth is thinner because of the walls beneath, and the different colour of the grass will reveal the layout of

the buried buildings; this is how remains of Roman camps have been discovered in England. A very good example of something similar took place in the Sudan, and is described by the British archaeologist Leonard Woolley:

At Wadi Halfa, in the northern Sudan, McIver and I had dug a temple and part of the Egyptian town, but, search the desert as we did for two months, we had failed to find any trace of the cemetery which must have been attached to the place. One evening we climbed a little hill behind the house to watch the sunset over the Nile; we were grumbling at our ill-luck when suddenly McIver pointed to the plain at our feet; its whole surface was dotted with dark circles which, though we had trampled over it day after day, we had never seen. I ran down the hill and the circles vanished as we came close to them, but, guided by McIver from

The temple to Athena at Paestum.

The acropolis at Selinunte. The columns of the north peristyle have been restored.

above, I made little piles of gravel here and there, one in the middle of each ring; and when we started digging there next morning our Arab workmen found under each pile the square, the rock-cut shaft of a tomb. The original grave-diggers had heaped the splinters of stone round the mouth of the shaft, and when they filled it up again a certain amount remained over. Four thousand years had produced a dead level of stone and gravel where the eye could distinguish no difference of arrangement or texture, but for the space of five minutes in the day the sun's rays coming at a particular angle brought out a darker tint in the stone which had been quarried from deeper underground—but, even so, the effect could only be seen from above and perhaps from a single point.

Animal behaviour may also be helpful to the observant archaeologist. A curious example of this is recorded by De Laet in his book *Archaeological Secrets*. Apparently an English archaeologist noticed that in an area populated by wild rabbits, parts of the ground were covered by a thin layer of earth and surrounded—but not occupied—by rabbits' burrows. His curiosity aroused, he started to dig and discovered that these parts were above some ruins covered by a thick layer of rock which the rabbits were unable to penetrate. In other words, the rabbits had left the archaeological zone intact, thus singling it out.

Toponymy, traditions and literary sources

The names of places are a fruitful source of information. It is a characteristic of many names that they remain unaltered, or at least stay recognizable, through the centuries: Rome, Athens and Jerusalem are known by the names they bore in antiquity. Apart from these obvious examples, there is Malatia, in Turkey, where excavations were conducted because of the name; and also Nabeul in Tunisia, which is an altered form of Neapolis, the name of an ancient Roman town.

Some names, though not derived directly from the ancient ones, are nevertheless an indication of antiquity because they recall aspects of past settlements. The name "Punta'e su coloru" ("Point of the serpents"), used for the hill on the site of the Phoenician city of Nora in Sardinia, derives from the presence there of an architrave of a small Egyptian temple with a frieze decorated with urea serpents, known by the local people since time immemorial. In Sicily the frequently encountered names Castellazzu and Cassero (the latter deriving from an Arab word meaning "fortress") almost always indicate the presence of ancient walls and towns, often pre-Greek. Turkish place-names containing *aslan* ("lion") are usually reminiscences of Hittite reliefs with lion-like figures.

Folklore and local traditions, if used with due care and discrimination, can also contribute to archaeological discoveries. Some themes are repeated with remarkable and significant frequency. One such theme is the story of a pot of gold buried under the altar of a church that has been destroyed, closely watched by the devil. The tale often refers to some now-ruined monument and can, therefore, be of help in finding it. Another commonly found story is about walls built by a race of giants: it usually indicates the presence of fortified town walls of some antiquity. Lastly the stories of magicians and ghosts often have some historical basis which, once realized, leads to the finding of antique objects.

As for the literary sources—that

is ancient and medieval texts which point to possible finds—it is clear that they are of primary importance, provided they are treated with discretion, and that their origins and authors are known. In fact any archaeological research must be preceded by thorough acquaintance with available literary sources, in order to become acquainted with all that has been written on the area in question, or alternatively as a guide in choosing sites to excavate, and also as an aid in the interpretation of the end results.

Aerial photography

Among modern techniques that have contributed to archaeological discoveries, aerophotography is the most important of all. The first attempts to take photographs from the air were made between 1930 and 1940, mainly for military purposes. The systematic air reconnaissance carried out by the Allied air forces on German-occupied countries during the Second World War have been most useful to archaeology as well, and are still valuable sources of information.

In certain conditions of light and at a suitable gradient, aerophotography shows features that would be invisible from any point on the earth's surface. For example, underground cavities such as tombs, canals, paved streets and squares, walls and embankments will affect moisture saturation in the grass cover, and therefore the colour of the grass itself. Aerophotography picks out the difference; and this was how Spina, the now famous Etruscan city at the mouth of the River Po, was located. The same method was used to locate the Roman fortifications of North Africa (the so-called *limes*) and the Phoenician and Carthaginian

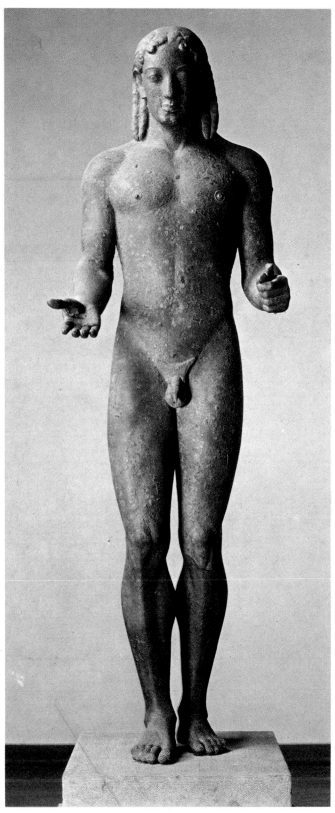

The Kouros. (Louvre Museum, Paris)

harbour works to be seen at Tiro, Mozia and Tharros.

The accepted opinion is that the best aerial photographs are those taken by the pilot himself, who, being in charge of the controls, is in the most favourable position to choose the angle from which the picture should be taken. In order to obtain useful views of irregular terrain, slanting shots are preferable; vertical shots are more suitable in bringing out the varied intensities of vegetation and to take panoramic views of the areas of interest. The best height from which to take aerial photographs varies according to the function they are required to serve. Large-scale pictures of small areas must be taken close up, while general views naturally need to be taken from a greater height. It is also important to choose the right time; if the ground is uneven and it is important to capture variation in height, the best times are early in the morning or at twilight, which favour slanting shots.

It may be as well to mention here another kind of photography often used in archaeology: underground photography, which will be described at greater length later on. It has been made possible by means of drills which penetrate the ground and insert a minute apparatus for flash photography inside the cavity below. This method is used when the area of investigation is already known; so it is more of a guide to excavation than a tool of original discovery.

Underwater exploration

Underwater exploration is another modern technique that has extended the possibilities of archaeological research. The glass masks, oxygen cylinders, compressed-air breathing-masks and flippers used for underwater fishing have become instruments of the archaeologist. There is also photographic apparatus that takes perfect pictures of whatever lies at the bottom of the sea, and plastic sheets on which a diver can write indelibly while under water. There are, too, vessels fitted with portholes and transparent walls from which one can see the bottom of the sea lit up by powerful lamps.

Underwater exploration has yielded rich results, especially in ancient locations that have been wholly or partly submerged as a result of earthquakes and such phenomena;

A fragment of a statue of the Ship of Mahdia. (Museum of the Bardo, Tunis)

such is the well-known centre of Baia, near Pozzuoli in Italy, which periodically yields statues of remarkable value. The discovery of ancient ships sunk near the coast, often with their entire cargo intact, is another feature of underwater archaeology: the most recent examples are the Phoenician ships discovered in the sea depths of Mozia, in Sicily, by British searchers led by Helen Frost. Incidentally, an additional incitement to the development of this branch of archaeology arose from the necessity of stopping thefts by frogmen of remains lying at the bottom of the sea.

A scientific organization for submarine research is emerging, particularly in Italy and France. There have been many recoveries of Greek and Roman ships off the Ligurian and Provençal coasts, conducted either by the submarine archaeological centre near the National Roman Museum of Albenga, under the direction of N. Lamboglia, or by the Museum of Aix-en-Provence, founded by F. Benoit. Furthermore, both in Italy and in France there are naval vessels specially fitted out for underwater research in the western Mediterranean.

Technology is of particular importance in preserving underwater finds. Long-submerged wood, for example, would soon fall to pieces if it were exposed to the air without first undergoing special treatment. The remedy is to immerse it in wax, which acts as a binding agent. This has to be done for a very long time—at least a year.

The technique was triumphantly used at the superb new Roskilde Museum in Denmark. Five Viking ships have been rescued from the Roskilde fjord, where they had been filled with stones and deliberately

C. M. Lerici, vice-president of the Lerici Foundation.

sunk in the eleventh century to shield the town from attack by pirates. To recover them, Danish archaeologists had to make an artificial dam round the sunken ships, pump out the water, photograph the site in detail, and then remove the ships piece by piece. Every plank then had to be immersed in wax, and later reshaped with the help of moulds. The work has been followed with intense interest throughout Scandinavia, since it has yielded information about the kind of Viking ships that made long journeys to Iceland, Greenland and even to North America.

Another Scandinavian triumph was the recovery of the *Vasa*, a seventeenth-century Swedish man-of-war, now on show at Stockholm.

One of the great events of British history—the defeat of the Spanish Armada which sailed to invade the country in 1588—provided the clues for an exciting find made in 1969. Battered by the English navy, and by gales in the Channel, the Armada fled northward, desperately trying to get back to Spain by going right round the British Isles. Many ships were lost in the attempt—more, in fact, than the English fleet managed to destroy. One, the *Girona*, was wrecked on the rocks of Lacade Point, on the Irish coast. Four hundred years later a Belgian underwater expert, Robert Stenuit, studied all the records of the Armada and, with the help of a team of divers, discovered the wreck—and a great treasure in golden doubloons and jewellery.

Physical, chemical and magnetic investigation

Geophysical techniques are still at an early stage in their application to archaeological research because they are expensive and call for complex appliances and highly trained specialists. These techniques were originally used in order to locate oil-fields and mineral deposits or in order to ascertain the nature of the subsoil before carrying out public works. One of the best known of these techniques is seismic prospecting. Lerici, one of the major exponents of modern applications of scientific and archaeological technology, says,

The seismic method is very well known as a technique already popular for research into hydrocarbons. It is based on the emission of waves under the ground, which are reflected or refracted when they meet a buried formation which may constitute an "anomaly", that is to say a variation in respect to the physical characteristics of the ground. . . . To this group belongs *sonic prospecting* and in general each investigation is based on the transmission of impulses. . . .

Chemical analyses are of great interest, based as they are on observation of the decomposition of organic substances. This method can only be employed with success where the human deposits are not too old—that is to say, where the soil components have not been subjected to changes that are too varied and complex to be classifiable. This explains why chemical analyses have been adopted with success in countries rich in medieval remains, such as Switzerland, Germany, Sweden and Holland, while they have found little application in Italy, Spain, Greece, Egypt and the Near East, where interest has been focused on much older civilizations.

Magnetic detectors, used in locating mineral deposits, are important in archaeology because they register the presence of metallic objects underground. We shall return to the subject of scientific instruments of detection; here it is only necessary to point out that detecting the presence of metallic objects tells us nothing about their

A potentiometer with electric voltmeter, built by the Lerici Foundation.

characteristic. Detectors locate ancient objects as well as sardine tins that have somehow become buried underground.

Surveying

Having dealt with the various methods which are used to detect the remains of ancient civilizations, we must now describe how large-scale surveys of known remains are organized, since such surveys are a pre-condition of intelligently co-ordinated work. The surveys are intended to provide the information with which the archaeological map of a country can be prepared. The most advanced example of surveying is the *Forma Italiae*, the vast plan carried out by the Institute of Topography at Rome University in order to produce an archaeological map of Italy. The way it works could be taken as a model for other such enterprises.

The work is shared by a number of scholars, often young graduates or undergraduates. Each of them is allotted an area, very small if it is in a densely populated region, relatively larger if it is out in the country. Preliminary preparations must be thorough—the surveyors must be able to recognize ancient remains, describe them, draw them, and mark them on the map. They must also be acquainted with everything in libraries and archives that has been written about the area assigned to them.

Once all the necessary preparations have been made, each surveyor goes on his way, armed with a ruler, a compass, a topographic map and a camera. If the objects to be surveyed are large monuments, two or three surveyors will be required. They will take with them metric rulers, spirit-levels, picket nails for measurement, and a special

apparatus called a "giraffe" for taking photographs from above. As far as transport is concerned, a jeep or some other strong and fast vehicle is most suitable.

Once photographed and recorded on special filing-cards, the remains will form part of a huge "collection" to be published later in a comprehensive and co-ordinated edition. This work of systematic research into our ancient heritage serves above all to safeguard it. It enhances its value, making possible the inclusion of such remains in town-planning schemes, and it establishes the favourable conditions needed for any organized excavation, which will have much of its work already done for it on the archaeological map of the region.

A proton magnetometer in operation.

CHAPTER 4

EXCAVATION

In the past, excavation was often a surprisingly casual affair. Before the days of passports and "treasure trove" laws, archaeology could be entirely a matter of private enterprise: if you were wealthy enough to hire labourers, there was little to stop you digging where and when you pleased. In the nineteenth century—the heyday of colonial empires—the European in the Middle East or Asia could usually buy cheap native labour and bribe or overawe the local authorities. At worst he could follow the example of Heinrich Schliemann, who broke his agreement with the Turkish government by smuggling out of the country a fortune in Trojan jewels and other precious objects. There was no Interpol in those days! By the 1920s archaeologists were more responsible and governments stricter—so that, for example, the Tutankhamun treasures excavated by Howard Carter remained Egyptian property and are still housed in the Cairo Museum.

Actual methods of excavation have also frequently left much to be desired. Of course, nothing could be expected of ancient tomb robbers, but eighteenth- and nineteenth-century "archaeologists" were little better when they became obsessed by dreams of hidden treasure. This is true of Schliemann, in spite of his Homeric inspiration and noble

The north entrance of the royal palace at Knossos. Heinrich Schliemann planned to excavate at Knossos, but he died before work could start.

49

vision of a rediscovered Troy. At Hussarlik he hacked his way down to what he mistakenly believed to be Homer's Troy; and though he discovered—and later smuggled out—the "Treasure of Priam", he also destroyed a vast amount of material in the layers above the Treasure.

Schliemann's contemporary, the French archaeologist Mariette, used dynamite to blast his way through ruins, destroying all sorts of evidence of ancient Egyptian life in his quest for the valuable and beautiful. And another offender was Lord Elgin, who transported to England great quantities of ancient Greek sculpture belonging to the Parthenon, the chief temple on the Athenian Acropolis. In removing the "Elgin Marbles" he also did a good deal of damage to the temple itself. The Greeks have never forgiven the "theft", though it can be said in Elgin's defence that both they and their Turkish rulers had done nothing to stop the Parthenon from falling into decay.

The proper principles of field archaeology were established by one of those unusual characters who so often appear in the history of this subject. Augustus Lane-Fox was a British military man who retired from the army for health reasons and inherited an estate at Cranborne Chase; a condition of the inheritance was that he change his name to Pitt Rivers. For twenty years, through the 1880s and 1890s, General Pitt Rivers excavated the prehistoric and Romano-British remains at Cranborne Chase. The conditions were ideal: he owned the area being excavated, he had plenty of money and time, and he had seen enough of excavations in Egypt and the Thames Valley to have understood the problems and formed his ideas.

Thus equipped, Pitt Rivers con-ducted a series of classic investigations, training his own assistants, being careful to destroy nothing, and recording, describing, measuring and labelling every item without making personal judgements about its value; he was sane enough to realize that what is insignificant to one generation may seem vital to the next. Models were made of the sites both before and after excavation, and models and finds were presented impeccably at a museum founded by Pitt Rivers at Farnham in Dorset; there it was possible for the visitor to understand not only what had been found but exactly where it had come from.

How does an archaeologist actually go about a dig? Let us look at the matter from the point of view of an archaeologist who has found an interesting site and wants to organize an excavation, with all that it involves. In reality things do not always begin in this way and continue as a logical progression: chance discoveries do sometimes occur, and then, just as in an emergency operation, unusual procedures are called for. But only by presenting a course of excavation, completely planned, will it be possible to examine the matter and its problems in all its aspects.

Funds and concessions

An archaeological excavation is, first of all, a considerable financial undertaking, and therefore quite a responsibility. It should be supported by one or more foundations, which can guarantee to set aside an adequate budget and ensure the employment of trained personnel. Such institutions may be government-sponsored bodies with regional branches, set up for research and conservation, in which case they

usually have their own archaeologists and their own organizations. But since they do not want to (and probably cannot) operate by themselves, they often invite the collaboration of outside archaeologists and institutions, granting them "concessions".

The "concession" is necessary because the land where the excavation is taking place is under the administration of a local authority as well as being within the jurisdiction of a particular State; hence permission to excavate is essential. In fact, during the course of the excavations, no one else will be allowed to operate on the same location. Of course, competent authorities do not give permission until they are fully satisfied that the excavators are both economically and scientifically sound.

On the other hand, if the land is privately owned, more complicated negotiations are necessary; but these are normally conducted by the authorities themselves. In some cases the only formality needed is the consent of the owners, with the proviso that no damage shall be done to cultivated land; should this occur, compensation will have to be given. Occasionally a rent is

The excavations at Phaestos in Crete.

fixed for the whole time spent on location. Finally, in more complicated cases, the authorities may decide to expropriate the owners with adequate compensation for any damage done.

Apart from the institutions already mentioned, university departments of archaeology are interested in excavations, since they are an indispensable element in the training of their students. There are also scientific and cultural institutions of various kinds that are called on to sponsor archaeological research. Finally, there are still a few private institutions in Europe, remnants of the patronage that played an essential part in archaeology a few centuries ago. In the U.S.A. such institutions are still flourishing, and handle huge sums of money. Because private institutions tend to be lured by the promise of sensational rather than historically valuable finds, funds from the State and public institutions are especially welcome by archaeologists as such funds provide a better guarantee of continuity and non-interference in the work of excavation, particularly if the excavation is a long one.

The inscription at the Temple of Augustus at Miseno.

Organization and equipment

Once permission to excavate has been obtained, the expedition must be organized. Obviously the central figure will be the director, who will generally have to shoulder scientific and administrative responsibility. Some expeditions may discriminate between the director *tout court* and the field director, who has the specific task of supervising the work on location. When the excavations are on a larger scale, they take place in various functionally independent areas, with directors on site responsible for their own section under a co-ordinating central control.

Much has been written on the essential qualities of a field director, but the best description is perhaps that given below:

First and foremost, the director must be a free agent, free from administrative detail. His primary and constant duty is to circulate from site to site and from workshop to workshop. Every section, in its latest manifestation, must be clearly in his mind's eye, and he must be familiar with every development in the hour-to-hour work of his team. If plans or sections are being made, he must himself ensure their adequacy; if his draftsman is drawing pottery, samples must be tested. His surveyor must be overlooked critically, his photographer utilized and supervised. Above all, he must familiarize himself with the groups of pottery as they lie on the tray beside the work or as they come from the wash, and he must occasionally check the marking of them. The indexes of small finds must be inspected daily. At some moment or moments during the day, he must examine the field notebooks of his supervisors. And he must keep his colleagues and employees constantly, in varying degrees, "in the picture", and ensure that they are, each of them, aware of the importance of their indivi-

dual contributions to the progress of the work.

Under the director there are many other workers who play important roles: the architect who surveys the discovered building; the draughtsman who registers the shape of each object of importance (sometimes, in less important excavations, the draughtsman's jobs are assigned to the architect); the photographer who makes records of the discoveries at each stage (though he is occasionally replaced by other members of the team, or even by the director himself); and the restorer, who is in charge of the first recon-

structions to protect the findings. Finally there are the assistants, mostly young students who look after particular sections or aspects of the excavation. All the best archaeologists have started their career under the guidance of more experienced workers.

In excavations far away from the base, and particularly in areas rich in inscriptions, the group will include an epigraphist who will examine and interpret any materials carrying written characters that come to light. Other specialists—numismatists, osteologists, palaeontologists—may be called in later, not necessarily during the excavation

Part of the excavation at Kerkouane in Tunisia, showing the mission house.

stage, in order to examine various types of evidence. Often their work entails elaborate analysis which can only be done in the laboratory.

As well as qualified staff, diggers must be found. People are often disappointed when they learn that the traditional picture of a solitary professor gingerly sifting through mounds of earth, does not bear up to reality. True, the archaeologist may dig, but when the enterprise is of a considerable size, it is still necessary to employ a sizeable number of workers, leaving the qualified staff to direct operations. Workers are usually recruited on the spot, for the obvious reasons that it is cheaper to do so and that their local knowledge may well prove of value. The choice of foreman is of utmost importance, since he provides a link between the workers and the director, for whom he may effectively substitute if necessary.

The equipment for excavations is of various kinds. The essential tools are those used to remove and sift earth: shovels, pickaxes, spades, hoes, brushes, sieves, etc. It is also necessary to have equipment to remove the remains found and the earth in which they were buried.

Where and how does an archaeological expedition take place? If the excavation is to take place near human habitations, it will be advantageous to take up residence there so as to have at hand services such as telephones, electric lighting, drinking water and provisions: the team can simply commute from built-up area to site by car or bus. When, on the other hand, the excavation is in a remote area, it is necessary to set up a camping site, or better still, to build small brick or prefabricated houses on the spot. This practice is particularly common where the excavators expect to return year after year. The greater

The main stone temple at Abu Simbel during salvage work. The temple was dedicated to Rameses II and his family.

The colossi of Rameses II at Abu Simbel.

is therefore essential for the expedition to bring a good supply of tinned food with them. Often water and electricity are not available, and the absence of these everyday commodities, normally taken for granted, can be sorely missed. Heat can be another serious problem. Apart from the fact that many excavation sites are in tropical regions, expeditions almost always take place in summer, since that is the time when attendents and lecturers are free.

In some parts of the world there are often serious dangers of disease and infection (carried, for example, by mosquitoes), or even death caused by poisonous animals such as snakes, tarantulas and scorpions. Bearing this in mind, it is clear that archaeology is a vocation, and one that may be partly motivated by a desire to escape from an over-comfortable and affluent society.

There are a number of other problems that must be taken into account—particularly in non-Western countries, where relations between the expedition and the local people, especially the workers, may bring difficulties. Problems of language, customs and habits are liable to crop up at any moment—for example, the well-known difficulties that occur in Asia and in Africa when European archaeologists come across a Muslem cemetery. In the past, archaeologists often rode roughshod over the feelings of the local people who, as well as having their own traditions, often resented the interference of strangers, fearing perhaps for their safety. Archaeologists who complain of lack of co-operation from local inhabitants, may well be paying the price for the arrogant behaviour of their predecessors. The very fact of throwing together workers in strange and uncomfortable conditions may

cost will be compensated for by the convenience of having permanent homes for equipment: a laboratory, a store for objects of minor importance or items that are too fragile to transport (ceramics, fragments of buildings and statues), a dark-room, and perhaps a room with a drawing-table for the architect. Some countries offer unusual living conditions: in Nubia, during the operations to save the monuments threatened by the water of the Nile, the archaeologists lived in boats on the river, going ashore only during working hours.

In spite of every precaution, there are always hardships in the life of an archaeologist, especially when he is in an isolated place away from his usual surroundings. Food may be scarce or unsuitable, and it create frictions which the director must resolve. But it is equally true that such exceptional circumstances may give rise to an unexpected solidarity and lasting friendships.

The excavations do not go on uninterrupted; on the contrary, it is preferable to work for short spells only, in order to devote the rest of the time to study and to arrange the publication of discoveries. The timing of the work is governed by the climate of the region. If possible, the party avoids working when temperatures are too hot or too cold, in rainy seasons and in other circumstances that may be unfavourable to successful operations. However, because the archaeologist's time is often limited, he may have to work in less than ideal conditions.

Methods and principles

As we have said, excavating begins only after a series of preliminary investigations has been carried out. Since information about suitable sites is plentiful, the final choice must depend to a considerable extent on local conditions. Sir Mortimer Wheeler, a famous British archaeologist, has said that the most favourable conditions for excavations are the all-round accessibility of the site, the possibility of full excavation and of ease of division into sections, and the possibility of preserving the remains for as long as possible in the best condition.

At the start of the operation, the expedition must have a survey map of the site, showing contours and elevations. First of all a co-ordinated reticle must be designed so as to enable the location of each object and monument to be identified in the correct section. This is known as "squaring". In a major excavation a big squaring is done, consisting of a hundred square metres broken up into smaller units of, say, ten metres. Each square is marked with numbers and letters so that it is immediately recognizable.

When choosing a method of "attacking" the site, it is essential to bear in mind the condition in which the archaeological remains may be found. Modern archaeology is based on the knowledge that the ruins of more than one past culture may have accumulated at various levels on a single site, forming a series of strata the age of which is related to the depth of the ground. Although the strata may vary in height and composition, and are sometimes separated, they form the framework of investigation within which ancient buried ruins may be located.

Only after accurate stratigraphic information has been obtained can work proceed. Circumstances may alter as work proceeds and therefore the course of the work cannot be predicted with certainty. In theory the director may decide to explore systematically a single stratum before going on to the one below it. In practice he usually starts by drilling in various places, on the basis of information already acquired, and then orders deeper excavations on the basis of what has been found. The excavation of squares or spaced segments of ground, taken in depth through the strata, has the advantage of "sampling" the ground, so improving the team's chances of identifying and concentrating on the areas of greatest interest.

Some problems on which archaeologists always disagree are met during the course of operations. There are never cut and dried answers to them since they are of the type that elicit different responses from different people, according to their age,

temperament and disposition. Sir Mortimer Wheeler has written knowledgeably on this. "There are no right ways of digging, but there are many wrong ways", he says. He has taken part in some controversies over his view of the drilling system as "an alternative to intelligent thinking and clear perception", while other archaeologists persist in recommending it. The controversy rages on a number of fundamental matters; for example, the relative advantages of horizontal and vertical excavation, and whether the centre of the periphery or the archaeological area should be given priority.

Horizontal excavation means the removal of a whole stratum before starting work on the next one. The advantage of this procedure is that it gives the most complete picture possible of what the stratum contains before work proceeds on the stratum beneath. Vertical excavation means examining a limited area in depth, in order to obtain evidence of the various phases that

can be found on the site, giving the archaeologist a good general picture of the situation before he examines any one level more extensively. Here, as elsewhere, the alternatives are not necessarily in conflict, and both methods may be used according to circumstances.

The second example is particularly relevant where the subject takes the form of a hillock or "tell". To excavate on the slope means to obtain very quickly and with the minimum of effort the stratigraphic information; to dig at the centre, on the other hand, gives a more reliable picture. Whichever method is preferred, it is vastly superior to a system which was widely used when archaeology was in its infancy —boring a gallery or tunnel into the mound, which destroys the archaeological remains without supplying any useful evidence.

The excavation of tombs presents a specific problem. Here stratigraphy is often very little help, while preserving the offerings frequently

Opposite: the remains of the Minoan palace at Phaestos in Crete.

The façade of a stone temple at Cyrene in Lybia.

59

buried with the dead is a vital and delicate task. The actual structure of the tomb must be carefully studied, and if it is underground the entrance must be found, the covering carefully removed, and entry effected in the same manner as the corpse-bearers and mourners. Above all, everything must be left in its place initially. Unfortunately, in Egypt, Etruria and most other places, the tombs had been violated long ago by treasure-hunters before they aroused archaeological interest. The famous Tomb of Tutankhamun is an exception, providentially discovered with all its precious objects

A detail of the vault of the Tomb of the Painted Animals at Caere, one of the major towns of maritime Etruria.

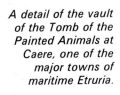

The Tomb of the Aeolian Capitals, also at Caere.

intact. Mural paintings are objects that need particular care, because the sudden changes of temperature and humidity that occur when the tomb is opened, often after many centuries, can cause rapid deterioration.

To return to excavation in general, the work is carried out by small teams, each in a well-defined section under the constant supervision of overseers. The earth is carefully removed to avoid damage to the emerging remains. Before removing any object discovered, a careful

Above: the stepped pyramid at Saqqara, 40 kilometres (25 miles) south of Egypt. The cemetery stretches for 7 kilometres ($4\frac{1}{2}$ miles) from the town.

Left: tomb painting from Thebes, one of the capitals of Egypt.

61

Athletes in action.
One of the paintings
in the Cardarelli Tomb
at Tarquinia, an
Etruscan town, north
of Rome.

note is made of the place and precise time of its recovery, Each phase of the operation is photographed, so that the conditions of the remains at each phase of their recovery is on permanent record—an important precaution since such phases and conditions are liable to change and the objects concerned will then never return to their original state. Equally essential, for recording events and the locations of discoveries, is the "journal" of the excavation, in which the archaeologist records in detail each development of the work and all the events accompanying it, such as interruptions due to external or internal circumstances or change of personnel involved in excavation.

Every object discovered must be cleaned up and restored as soon as possible, preferably in the expedition's own laboratory. It is numbered immediately, and a metal or wooden label is fixed to it, or the number is simply written on it in ink. A brief description, setting out the place of origin, is entered on to filing-cards, to which a photograph is also affixed. The filing-cards are indispensable, once the expedition is over, for study and for the publication of the findings.

Yet another problem is the removal of the shifted earth. Obviously it cannot be left in the excavation area, as it would obstruct other excavations. As a solution, small wagons on rails are used. The debris

is removed along the rails to a zone that is archaeologically sterile. Often this zone is suitable for cultivation, and the debris may be useful to farmers; the lava which buried the cities of Pompeii and Herculaneum turned out to be excellent fertilizer.

At the end of each dig the site must be closed, fenced round and provided with guards, usually recruited on the spot. The material which cannot be removed must be adequately protected against the weather, while the movable material is packed and taken to a suitable museum. Of course there are other problems connected with archaeological expeditions operating far from their base, but we shall look at them later in the book.

The Discoveries' destination

A fundamental principle of modern archaeology is that each country has exclusive property rights over works of art and any other objects brought to light during excavation, irrespective of the nationality of the archaeologists concerned or the ownership of the land on which the dig takes place. In practice the principle may be waived to a greater or lesser extent in order to satisfy all such interested parties. Such compromises are common sense. No restrictions at all would probably lead to extensive removals of relics from the place of their discovery, while an absolute prohibition on the export of finds might well deter archaeologists from mounting expeditions at all.

As far as the owners of the site are concerned, in the past it was often the practice to hand over some of the finds to them. Now they are offered a sum of money as compensation for damage, a practice that is to be preferred not so much for commercial reasons as because of the historical and artistic importance of the remains. Rewards are also given to people who find archaeologically valuable objects, whether on their own property or not. This is aimed at discouraging illicit sales and export, two evils of which we shall speak in another chapter.

European countries insist that all material discovered on the expedition must be handed over *in toto* to the authorities, although there may be a few exceptions in practice. The situation is less well defined in other countries, particularly those in the Near East. Israel, Jordan and Egypt who allow expeditions to acquire substantial parts of the material, and in Nubia, temples have been taken to pieces and rebuilt abroad. Much depends, of course, on the existence of "doubles"—objects which are duplicated and which may be given away without depleting the archaeological heritage.

In other words, the time of more-or-less legal plundering, which characterized some famous discoveries of the past, is over. Study of the finds and preparation of publications—activities obviously reserved for the members of the expedition—is much preferred to possessing the finds themselves. Indeed, examining objects discovered and publishing the results of the expedition are the first concerns of reputable archaeological enterprises, and without this concern excavation could be a waste of effort and even harmful.

A golden earring discovered at Tharros.

CHAPTER 5

CONSERVATION AND PUBLICATION

The basic need to conserve every-thing found during an excavation is one of the greatest problems facing the archaeologist. At times this problem arises even before the discovery is made. The simplest obvious example is that of a painting on the wall of an ancient tomb. It is imperative to put immediately into practice the necessary pro-tective measures in order to avoid irreparable damage from humidity and a sudden change of tempera-ture. Let us suppose that under-ground photography reveals the existence of such a painting before the excavation starts. Obviously the method and timing of the excavation will be geared to this knowledge. Furthermore, a painting which is exhibited on an archaeo-logical site, or in a museum, will not necessarily be exempt from either wear and tear or damage; so in all cases it appears to be very important that a trust be formed to take care of archaeological finds.

Restoration and conservation of the archaeological heritage are two of the great problems of our times. The examples cited above are only the natural elements in the problem. There are also unnatural elements, such as wars and public works, the most sensational modern ex-ample of which is the construction of the Aswan High Dam in Egypt, which stimulated a great inter-national effort to save the ancient temples threatened by the waters.

In addition to conservation, in the wide sense of the word, there is the problem of restoration—one of the most complex and con-troversial subjects in art and archaeo-logy. For example, a head found separated from the torso of a statue to which it belongs, and to which it can easily be rejoined, will obviously be put back on. But when an object is fragmented into a thousand pieces, when many of the pieces are missing, is it really meaningful—and to what extent is it possible or useful—to

Opposite: a detail of the wall painting in the Temple of Horemheb in the Valley of Kings at Thebes.

Photographing the interior of a tomb with a periscope probe.

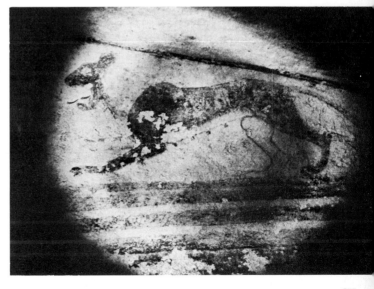

Opposite: the Ficorini cist. Cists were stone chests containing human burials or cremated remains. (National Museum of Villa Giulia, Rome)

Two bronze relics from Melfi. Above: a tripod. Below: a mirror with the handle shaped as a human form.

return it partly to its original state?

Another question of some importance is *where* archaeological material should be preserved. The most obvious alternatives are to preserve it on the site or to transport it to a museum. If the choice falls on a museum, the next question is, what sort of museum? Local and specialized, or general and centralized? Add to these the inevitable questions about how the material should be displayed, what part of it should be held in the reserves, sent out in periodical exhibitions, etc., and it becomes clear that successful excavations by no means end the archaeologist's problems.

Publication is another, ultimately

more permanent form of conservation. Until a record of the discoveries is published, they cannot be properly studied by interested scholars; and it is this study which must be considered the final goal of the whole process of discovery. But, of course, there are different ways of publishing; the archaeologist who takes an active part in the expedition has a duty to put forward all the necessary data, showing the nature, methods, times and circumstances of the discoveries.

Protection and conservation

Excavation, Sir Mortimer Wheeler has justly remarked, is always a form of destruction. This means that from the moment the excavation begins it is necessary to adopt all possible measures to protect

Relief showing Assyrian archers. (Louvre Museum, Paris)

the remains. Where the objects are portable, the solution is relatively simple: they are photographed at the time of discovery, and every detail of their condition, and the circumstances in which they were found, is recorded. They can then be removed right away, at first to the expedition's store, later to a laboratory or museum. Ceramics are a good example of portable objects, although they have special features. The washing of fragments of pots or figures, their classification and (where possible) temporary reassembly is one of the most onerous tasks in any excavation, and is often entrusted to young and eager assistants.

Once transportable objects have been removed from the site, they require special treatment for their preservation, though the nature of the treatment will vary according to the nature of the article concerned. Metal objects will be placed in a special fluid to protect them from corrosion. Statues will be cleaned in suitable solutions and then coated with wax diluted with certain chemicals, or alternatively brushed with lime-water mixed with casein. Bones will be first of all freed from encrustation and then strengthened with resin or gum. Wood will be treated by fumigation or with chemical solutions against insects and fungi, and holes will be filled with wax. These are only brief examples of the technical work which must be done—and done quickly—in order to preserve transportable objects.

The preservation of remains that cannot be removed is more complicated. Walls are often unsafe, and excavation may destroy them if they are not strengthened and supported. But even after such operations are carried out, external agents are a constant danger; water,

The depository in the National Museum of Capodimonte in Naples.

Below: the restoration room.

Cleaning the Cardarelli Tomb at Tarquinia with potassium nitrate.

for example, can seep through cracks in walls and freeze during the winter, destroying the walls when it melts again. Equally dangerous are micro-organisms which multiply in humid conditions, corroding the stones.

Faced with such situations, the archaeologist must act vigorously. If necessary, a monument in danger of collapsing will be taken down and rebuilt in another place. When, on the other hand, this is not possible or desirable, it is necessary to isolate the buildings from the ground by means of reinforced-concrete slabs, and to treat the stone with a substance that will destroy corrosive agents. As for water which may have filtered into walls, there are aeration and purification systems that combat the destructive effects of moisture and atmosphere. There are also other measures to be taken which are straightforward and in a sense elementary, but quite effective, such as covering exposed areas with sheet roofing, encasing objects with glass walls (which do not impede vision but exclude atmospheric agents), and in extreme cases carrying out a provisional reburial of the discovered objects.

Treating the wall paintings in a reassembled Etruscan tomb.

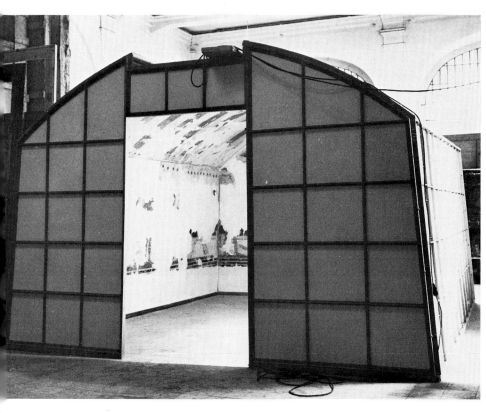

The paintings in this reconstructed Etruscan tomb have been externally supported.

Renovated paintings from an Etruscan tomb.

Restoration

Preservation and restoration are closely connected, as is fairly obvious, but with restoration problems arise when some parts of the discovered object are missing. The question is of theoretical significance even before arising in practice: should ancient remains be left as they are? In other words, is it a good thing to put them together so that they are as they were in the past or is the only authentic course of action to let well alone?

Nowadays opinion generally favours restoration, provided that the object being restored will be recognizable in the end. For example,

The Temple of Zeus at Olympia.

if the fragments of a statue are found it should be reassembled only if it can be done accurately and provided that any missing pieces are replaced with slightly different materials, so that in close examination the original fragments can be discerned from the modern duplicates. However, the use of replacements must not spoil the appearance of the statue.

Paintings also require special attention. Whenever possible, it is advisable for the excavators to *fix* them there and then. Fixing ensures their preservation, using techniques directed against the action of atmospheric conditions. When this is not possible, it is necessary to resort to

The restored façade of
the Temple of Aphaea
at Aegina.

The temple at Antas
after restoration.

The Forum in Rome.
The temple was
dedicated to Saturn.

"peeling"—that is, the removal of a thin layer of colour and plaster from the wall by transferring it on to canvas, using special adhesive solutions; this layer is later removed from the canvas and taken on a special stretcher to a museum, or to wherever the paintings will be kept with proper care. Usually, walls and columns are reconstructed in order to show them as they were in the past. This practice, which at one time would have been rejected because of a romantic preference for "picturesque" ruins, is widely adopted today, though the approach is not the same in all cases. Sometimes a "complete" reconstruction is made, even when a good deal of the work is speculative to the point of

The ruins of the Domus Flavia in Rome.

The small trellis-work house at Herculaneum near Naples.

"making up" the missing parts. As a general criterion for restoration, this is not wholly acceptable. A much better principle is to restore columns and monuments as far as possible, completing them only where this is necessary to harmonize the effect, leaving the new elements clearly visible.

Exhibitions

The ever-growing popularity of exhibitions presents a serious responsibility to the organizers, since success or failure may depend on the effectiveness of presentation. Even the choice of museums is much wider than it was a few years ago. Exhibitions may be held in the open air or indoors, on or away from the site of discovery, presented in a variety of ways.

When the exhibition is in the open air, in the place where the discovery was actually made, the result can be a permanent monumental complex such as the Roman Forum. In the last few years the idea of creating

A painted Lucan stele from Paestum.

A superb example of Lucan painting also from Paestum.

The gilded hall of the Poldi Pezzoli Museum in Milan.

The Pasagno Gallery in Italy. The plaster casts on display are by Canova, the Italian neo-classical sculptor.

archaeological parks has developed —that is to say, the arrangement of the ruins in landscapes under adequate supervision, with the idea of educating the public and encouraging tourism. For obvious reasons the establishment of such parks usually takes place at the great centres of antiquity such as Pompeii, Cerveteri, ancient Ostia, Agrigento and Selinunte.

In such important areas we often find an Antiquarium, which is a small local museum with a collection of objects found on the site that are small but of considerable significance. The establishment of the Antiquarium allows the public to see as many remains as possible in a systematic manner, in the spot where the cities of antiquity flourished.

Naturally, museums have their uses too. The authorities have two

alternatives: either to increase the large, already-existing collections by a policy of concentration, or to decentralize by favouring local collections. In both cases there are advantages and disadvantages. The large museum has proper facilities for cataloguing, for exhibitions and for study, which the small museum lacks. On the other hand, the smaller museum tends to have a character and closely defined collections that are in many ways more satisfying for the general public. There seems no doubt that the trend is towards decentralization, which also makes some part of the past more immediately available to a greater number of people.

How should museum exhibits be arranged? Here too there are various ideas and methods. The exhibition may adhere to chronological criteria or to typological and geographical ones. In some museums the material is increased to its maximum, in others it is selected in order to give a clearer, more effective impression, leaving a great number of objects in store (but ideally giving access to the public!). Exhibits in glass cases

The Solomon R. Guggenheim Museum in New York. Designed by Frank L. Wright, this controversial building houses paintings by Chagall, Léger, Cézanne, Renoir and Manet among many others.

should always be clearly labelled, but unfortunately this is not always done. (There are still many large museums with annotations in one language only—that of the host country—which is often a language not widely known.) On the whole, however, remarkable advances have taken place in the arrangement of show-cases: they are better designed, clearer and lighter than in the past.

Museums which specialize in what they collect, such as Egyptian relics, medals, or coins are of particular interest as are didactic museums. These are oriented towards teaching and are mainly found in universities. They display tracings and drawings, and copies of material for study purposes.

Publication

It is a duty of the utmost importance for the archaeologist to publicize the results of his excavation. Most of us are likely to assume that doing so would be a source of intense satisfaction to him, but, in fact, there is no duty less honoured than this one. Many expeditions have not published their findings at all, some have done so only partly and, in general, there are more unpublicized excavations than publicized ones. This is one of the major sins in archaeology, and the more so since archaeologists who do not publish will usually refuse as well to permit others to publish their material. In such circumstances, it would have been better not to excavate at all, leaving open the possibility of a future discovery that would be adequately made known.

Naturally archaeologists find plenty of reasons to explain this state of affairs: the urgency of other work, the difficulty of quickly assessing some of the discoveries, the lack of an immediately available publisher, and so on. However, the paragraphs that follow give an outlined procedure that all archaeologists should, and easily could, pursue.

Archaeological reports are usually divided into two sections. The first is a concise account that is published yearly after each campaign. These annual reports are of historical importance, for they describe the chief excavation areas, showing, with suitable illustrations, the most exciting discoveries. In such reports there is not, and should not be, any pretensions to completeness since later excavations may very well modify early judgement. The intention is to record the evolution of the work, registering data which might at any time become invaluable. Preliminary reports usually take the form of articles, written by, or under the direction of, the head of the expedition.

The systematic presentation of discoveries is reserved for the final reports, which are published once excavation has ended for good. Here it is no longer a matter of articles but of volumes, in which the documentation will have to be as exhaustive as possible. The volumes will generally be divided into a number of categories, dealing with monuments, architectural remains, statues, paintings, ceramics and other artefacts. Accurate catalogues will be compiled for each category, accompanied by an attempt at evaluation which will start, though it will certainly not conclude, the integration of the discoveries into the common heritage. Each member of the expedition is responsible for some part of the publication, thus linking his name with the definitive record of the achieved mission.

An idea recently put forward in Italy is that a period of five years after a discovery should be fixed by law as the archaeologist's "copyright"; if he has not published his findings within this time, the discovered material should become common property which anyone can study or publish. This plan shows how seriously the problem of publication should be regarded.

It reinforces the lesson quoted by André Parrot: "it is better to be open to criticism than to be like the dragon in the legend, jealously keeping watch over a useless treasure in his lair".

The Plaster Cast Gallery in the Institute of Archaeology in Rome.

83

CHAPTER 6

UNKNOWN WRITINGS
AND LANGUAGES

Although epigraphy, the study of ancient inscriptions, is a science in its own right, its points of contact with archaeology are manifold. When excavations bring to light ancient inscriptions, epigraphical techniques are at once brought to bear on them. Deciphering and interpreting such evidence is an essential part of archaeological research, not only for general cultural reasons but also because the dating of inscriptions can be an essential element in establishing the chronology of an entire stratum, settlement or civilization.

We are not concerned here with the problems and the methods of epigraphy as such, just because it is a separate science (not to mention the fact that problems and methods vary enormously with the languages and inscriptions concerned). We shall instead concern ourselves with those aspects of the subject that are directly connected with archaeology —the deciphering and interpretation of writings and unknown languages unearthed by excavations.

The epigraphist, confronted with an obscure inscription, is like a counter-espionage agent who has gained possession of a message in cipher. The methods adopted for the interpretation of inscriptions coincide in some respects to those used in deciphering a code, although

the epigraphist is luckier in that the document with which he is confronted, although unintelligible to him, is not intentionally obscure or misleading.

The terms of the problem

When the epigraphist tackles the problem of an ancient inscription in an obscure language, he must first define the nature of its unintelligibility. There are three possibilities: that the script is known, but not the

Opposite: Early Egyptian Hieroglyphics.

The statue of Gudea dedicated to the god Ningursu. The statue was discovered during excavation work at Lagash, one of the most important centres during the Sumerian period. (Louvre Museum, Paris)

language; that the language is known, but not the script; or that both language and script are unknown. The situation in the first case is self-evident: the epigraphist can read the inscription but does not understand it. At first glance the other two cases seem effectively the same; but they diverge if the epigraphist is successful in deciphering the script, for then everything is relatively straightforward if the language emerging is of a known type. If it is an unknown language however, the full solution may still

be many years away.

An example of the first case is the Etruscan language. It has been already deciphered, and is in fact a script of the Greek type which is very readable indeed. But long and patient study has failed to reveal the meaning of more than a few words and some grammatical structures. Etruscan does not belong to any known linguistic group and the prospects of understanding it properly seem small.

The inscriptions left by the Greeks who colonized Cyprus be-

tween the end of the second millennium B.C. and the beginning of the first, are a good example of the second case, where the language is known but not the way of writing it. These Greeks wrote their language not in their own characters, but in the syllabic characters used by the natives and dating back to Mycenaean times. Another example is the famous Linear B, the syllabic Mycenaean script which was deciphered in a way that will be described a little later. It was in fact used to write a language which was an archaic form of Greek.

Finally, as an example of the third situation, there is the case of Egyptian hieroglyphics, which the French archaeologist Champollion succeeded in deciphering without knowing either the script or the language for which it stood. In such a situation there is little hope of solving the problem unless a bilingual text is discovered, that is an inscription that gives the same text in two languages (and scripts), one of which is known. Even in such instances the problems are far from over, but the possibility of a solution is at least seen to exist.

Method and criteria

Neither a "discoverer's handbook" nor a "decipherer's handbook" exist. The situations vary and the possible ways of approaching an obscure document are legion. Furthermore, a large part is played by two unclassifiable factors: ability and luck. Nevertheless a few general criteria and preliminary points are worth mentioning in order to demonstrate how the epigraphist goes about his job.

First of all he must establish the direction of the writing. When we examine any text, the last line (of a page, or of paragraphs on the page) rarely fills the whole space available. So if the spaces are on the right, it means that the writing goes from left to right, as in our form of writing, which is aptly called "dextrorse". If on the other hand there are one or more spaces on the left, it means that the writing goes in the opposite direction and is therefore "sinistrorse", as is the case in some Semitic languages such as Arabic and Hebrew.

Another point to clarify is the way in which words are separated from one another. This is often indicated by a hyphen, by a dot, or by a blank space (as is the case in European languages). The division of the text into words allows the epigraphist to work out the average length of the words themselves and perhaps the average number of words in a sentence. This may be essential to the understanding of the type of language in question. In the Semitic languages, for example, only consonants are written down, so that there are far fewer letters in each word than in the Indo-European group of languages, in which both vowels and consonants are represented.

A third fundamental point is the importance of discovering the total number of letters used in a script. This can be clearly defined, provided a fairly long text is examined. For example, an alphabetical script does not have more than about thirty letters; therefore a text which remains within these limits is likely to be an alphabet. If, on the other hand, there are many more letters, then we are certain to be dealing with an ideographic or syllabic writing, or a combination of both. Such were the scripts of the great Near Eastern civilizations of Egypt and Mesopotamia, both of which flourished long before the Phoenicians invented the alphabet.

Once these fundamentals are established, the epigraphist must go over every item in his inscription with meticulous attention, find out where it comes from, if possible define it, and fit it into the known context—in fact, do all that is necessary to establish the linguistic group to which it belongs. An ancient tablet from Knossos, for example, will be written in Linear A or B, which were the two scripts common on the island of Crete during the second millennium. An ancient Mesopotamian tablet, on the other hand, will probably be written in Sumerian or in Akkadian, and certainly in a language belonging to the group using cuneiform script.

Deciphering

After he has dealt with the points mentioned above, the decipherer will proceed to the interpretation of the unknown text. The most difficult situation, as we have seen, is one in which both language and script are obscure. Some kind of starting-point is essential, the most typical

Pl. IV.

Tableau des Signes Phonétiques
des écritures Hiéroglyphique & Démotique des anciens Égyptiens

Lettres Grecques	Signes Démotiques	Signes Hiéroglyphiques
A		
B		
Γ		
Δ		
E		
Z		
H		
Θ		
I		
K		
Λ		
M		
N		
Ξ		
O		
Π		
P		
Σ		
T		
Υ		
Φ		
Ψ		
X		
Ω		
TO TA		

Table of phonetic signs created by Jean François Champollion the Egyptologist who became keeper of the Egyptian collection in the Louvre Museum in Paris.

being a bilingual inscription; that is to say, the identical text reproduced in two versions, one in a known script, and one in the script to be deciphered. Such inscriptions are not rare, particularly in official documents, and in some surviving examples there are even texts written in three languages.

The possession of a bilingual text is of fundamental importance to the decipherer since it reveals in advance the contents of the text to be interpreted. Even so, a hint— some kind of specific connection between words in the two texts—is essential. It is usually supplied by proper names, which remain recognizable in different languages or over extended periods of time. Hence the epigraphist will take as his starting-point the proper names in the known parts of the bilingual text and will try to identify them in the unknown part.

The most famous of all examples of this kind of work is Egyptian hieroglyphics, which Champollion was able to interpret after the discovery of the Graeco-Egyptian

stelae at Rosetta. The name of King Ptolemy was the first to be recognized, partly thanks to the help of an oval ring framing the names of pharaohs in Egyptian hieroglyphs. This ring is known as the "cartouche". Another case is the cuneiform inscription, which the English Assyriologist Rawlinson interpreted using the trilingual inscription in ancient Persian, Babylonian and Elamitic, engraved on a rock wall at Behistum near Persepolis. His task was made easier by the fact that the name of the king appeared here as it often did at the beginning, in the inscription "Darius great King, King of Kings, King of the Nations, son of Istape, Achemenide."

Proper names are of course only a starting-point. Once the value of a few signs is found, the epigraphist looks for them in all the words in which they occur and then proceeds on this basis to construct hypotheses concerning the rest of the signs. The verification of the accuracy of the hypotheses is the agreement that should exist between the results it gives and the translated text. More generally, the fact that the hypotheses are not mutually inconsistent, and that the translations they yield make sense, will speak powerfully in their favour.

Sometimes, though, it has been possible to decipher an inscription without even the aid of the bilingual texts. This happened to the script used in Ugarit, the Syrian city discovered in 1929. The French researcher Virolleand, faced with the task of deciphering hundreds of clay tablets found in the city's archives, first of all observed that the signs, a series of cuneiform inscriptions of the Mesopotamian type, were about thirty in all and must therefore form an alphabet. Furthermore the words, separated from one another by hyphens, consisted on average of three or four letters each. Obviously, then, the language was a Semitic one, since this is the average number in other Semitic writings. Naturally the fact that the site was in Syria suggested that Ugaritic would be a Semitic language and script.

The interest of Virolleand's inquiry is such as to warrant telling the rest of the story. After the preliminary observations already described, he took as his starting-point a group of bronze objects on which the same signs constantly appeared. It therefore seemed reasonable to suppose that these represented the name of the owner. The same letters appeared at the beginning of a tablet also, preceded by an extra sign. Virolleand guessed that the tablet was a letter addressed to the man in question and that the extra sign was the letter *l*, which in Semitic means "to" and is used to start a correspondence. On the basis of this guess, Virolleand drew up a list of words with the letter *l*, which was found to appear very frequently as the last part of a word; it was thought that this word was "Baal", the name of the most important god. And if "Baal" was right, the first letter was *b*, which in Semitic means "in" . . . and so from one hypothesis to another, until the Ugaritic language was deciphered.

Another classic feat of deciphering was the solution of Linear B, a form of writing used on Mycenaean tablets of the second millennium B.C. Here the script was much more complex than the Ugaritic one because it contained a much larger number of signs, a fact that indicated it was both a syllabic and an ideographic alphabet. After a lot of guesswork the British linguist

The Rosetta stone which gave the key to deciphering Egyptian hieroglyphics. It was discovered by Napoleon's army in Egypt in 1799 and seized by the British in 1801. (British Museum, London)

THE ROSETTA STONE

Michael Ventris succeeded in deciphering it by applying a method commonly used in cryptography—and more or less in the way it was applied in espionage. He compiled a series of statistic tables, indicating the signs and their position. He guessed that three signs corresponded to vowels, because they recurred mainly at the beginning of a word. He provisionally identified a suffix with the conjunction "and". And on the basis of analogies with the Cypriot script he established some values. Then he tried to find the names of localities. He finally succeeded when he tried to interpret the results at which he had arrived through Greek, of which—as we have seen—the tablets record an ancient form.

Sometimes deciphering work has been started successfully and then halted by an error committed during the work. It is enough to make one mistake in attaching hypothetical meaning to some signs to ruin the whole system. Other factors, such as misleading similarities between various signs and terms, may lead to incorrect interpretations. The only meaningful verification comes from the results—only a coherent account of the texts proves that the

task has been successfully accomplished. Doubts remain about small texts. For example, the attempts to interpret Sinaitic writing, typical of inscriptions of the early second millennium B.C., have met with frustration. Some progress has been made, but it has been curtailed by the scarcity of the material.

In conclusion, deciphering unknown languages and inscriptions requires a very extensive linguistic preparation, an exceptional knowledge of cryptography, a great deal of patience and intuition, and the essential element in all human enterprises—luck.

Opposite: the steps at the Tripylon at Persepolis. Above: the gates of the Tripylon showing the king on his throne.

CHAPTER 7

FORGERY AND
ILLICIT TRADE

As explained in the first chapter of this book, interest in archaeology is no longer confined to a restricted élite of specialists, but is displayed by an ever-growing public. This is without doubt a good thing, since it promotes the flow of public and private funds into research, field-work and the preservation of existing monuments. Nevertheless, the enthusiasm for archaeology has some negative aspects as well. The possibility of shady but just-about-legal business deals, and the selfish mania for private collecting, with its naïveté and its dangers, encourage clandestine excavations, illicit speculations and forgery, and can bring archaeology into disrepute.

Forgery has its precedents in antiquity. There is an ancient Egyptian papyrus illustrating methods used to imitate precious stones by means of coloured glass. Pliny and Vitruvius describe how to simulate colours; Seneca refers to laboratories where jewels were made. All this shows that attempts to manufacture items of spurious antiquity have flourished throughout the ages, exploiting the enthusiasm for ancient and valuable objects. In addition we must bear in mind that it is by no means always easy to distinguish between what is genuine and what is imitation. Reputable museums have for years displayed, as originals, works that were later declared false beyond doubt; and famous scholars have pronounced expert judgements and opinions which they afterwards had reason to regret.

Naïveté and sheer ignorance on the part of amateurs are the essential conditions in which forgeries can flourish. The Latin poets hold up to ridicule the credulity of people who deluded themselves that they possessed objects which had belonged to famous people: for example the cup that had been used by Nestor, or the basin in which Sirius washed his feet. In the Middle Ages there were thousands of false relics, revered in churches and cathedrals and sold to the pious of all classes. During the Renaissance hoaxing became popular. One of the most famous was perpetrated by Michelangelo, whom Lorenzo de' Medici had commissioned to make a statue of Cupid. Michelangelo made the statue and then had it buried; later he "discovered" it and for a time passed it off as a Roman work. Later, paintings became particularly prone to forgery. They (more than any other objects) are at the mercy of art forgers, being the most expensive to buy and easiest to falsify of all the arts. But the definition of what is false is not always clear and the responsibility is not all one-sided. This is a subject that must be investigated at greater length.

The Etruscan necropolis at Orvieto.

The nature of forgeries

The unquestionable forgery is carried out in full consciousness and for the sake of gain. The forger imitates an ancient work and then tries to sell it, claiming that it is genuine. The matter becomes more complicated when the craftsman to whom the work was entrusted carries it out in good faith, perhaps on the orders of unscrupulous men who later sell it at a huge profit, passing off the craftsman's careful copy as a genuine antique. In other words, copies and imitations may be perfectly legitimate; forgery exists when there is a deliberate intention to deceive.

Legitimate imitations and copies are made and acquired for study for teaching, and even for simple personal pleasure. Hoaxes too, though often cruel, are not subject to legal sanctions unless they are done to gain money. One notable victim was Professor Beringer of Würzburg, who during one of his excavations found some wonderful fossils shaped like flowers, animals and stars. As a result he wrote a Latin dissertation in which he asserted the authenticity and praised the value of his discovery. Only later did the truth come to light; the fossils had been manufactured by his students and buried in a suitable place to make him believe that they were immensely old.

The various degrees of forgery are matters of considerable complexity. It is possible to copy an antique object with modern material, or to adapt an already old object so that it appears still older or else part of some more admired group or category. Likewise "forgery" may consist of altering an existing signature or adding one that is not there at all. To understand the plausibility of many forgeries one must remember the methods used by sculptors, painters and craftsmen in the past. Their pupils worked with them in their workshops, often finishing a work just roughed out by the master. Later on the master might re-touch the work. And so, many objects cannot be assessed as single creative arts, but show signs of the work of several hands—one or more of which could be a forger's.

How forgers work

Paintings invite forgery most strongly because of the high prices they command and the easy market they find. If the painting to be forged is on wood, the forger must get hold of genuinely ancient material, for new wood can be detected by chemical analysis. As for canvas, it is made to look old by boiling it and then bleaching it in the sun. Sometimes a new canvas is glued on to an old one, which will remain visible at the back of the picture, suggesting its antiquity, while the new one at the front is covered with paint; or else the forger may use a really ancient picture, but one of little value, scraping away or washing off the original painting and replacing it with an "Old Master". The forger must have a considerable knowledge of pigments and their history, since some colours did not exist in the past, while others were prepared in a different way from that now used. The cracks which appear in the surfaces of old paintings may be induced artificially by exposing them to high temperatures, or by applying layers of varnish which dry off at different speeds. Bubbles, mould and layers of dust on the surface can also be induced artificially.

Forgery in sculpture seems to be less frequent. To find ancient

material is almost impossible, and forgers, therefore, usually work with new materials which they "age" artificially. Marble surfaces are corroded by acids, calcification is faked by using oxyhydrogen flame, and skilful chisel hammering produces fractures which may plausibly pass for ancient ones. Patinas can be produced on bronze only by chemical means. Finally, burying statues, even for a relatively short period, is useful in giving them a coating of earth, which makes them look antique.

Jewellery forgeries are very common and very difficult to discover, mainly because it is hard to thoroughly examine silver and gold without damaging them; their well-known pliability protects the forger. Their high value, and the fact that they are small and easily portable, makes most forms of jewellery tempting to the private buyer and even, on occasion, to the museum. At the end of last century, for example, the Louvre Museum in Paris purchased the so-called "Saitapharnes tiara", a presumed work of Graeco-Saitic jewellery from the third century B.C. which later was found to be the work of a contemporary Russian artist.

Also easily faked, and subject to imitation at all times and in all countries, are coins. While many forms of imitation require technical skill and talent, coins can be faked either by obtaining new moulds from the original ones or by using the original moulds and an authentic metal made up from a cheaper alloy. This last system has been used by many a government during times of shortage of precious metal.

Pottery has been faked throughout history, recorded and unrecorded. Many well-known modern firms produce Etruscan vases which are sold to amateur collectors, who are inclined to be gullible, and in any event find it difficult to obtain valuations of their proposed purchases from reliable sources. But the phenomenon is not limited to amateurs. A few decades ago a series of ceramics believed to be extremely ancient and originating from Palestine was bought by museums in Paris, Berlin and London. The seller was an antique dealer who declared that he had acquired the objects at the place of origin. What he said was true in a sense, but the place of origin later turned out to be Apulia, in Italy.

Human remains do not escape forgers either. In 1953 the *British Museum Journal* revealed that a famous skull, which for about forty years had been considered a point of reference in the study of anthropology, was in fact a forgery. This was the Piltdown skull, so called from the locality, near Newhaven, where the skull had been "discovered"; in fact it had been made from a mixture of human and monkey bones. Another example has occurred in Ecuador, where mummified human skulls have been successfully copied, using monkeys' heads.

How forgers are found out

The forger may be well equipped, but so is the scientist. Forgers are generally found out and forgery is generally recognized as such. Perhaps the most important of all methods of detection is a thorough examination of the materials used—canvases and colours for pictures, stone and metals for statues, ceramic ware for vases, and so on.

Microscopic examination can enlarge particles of the material examined up to hundreds and even thousands of times, revealing its structure and its stratification. Thus it is possible to differentiate between what is and what is not artificial. Corrosions caused by acids, calcination obtained by oxyhydrogen flame, and false patinas can be detected if there is a layer of dust between them and the surface on which they rest. Spectrographic examinations, particularly X-rays, give equally conclusive results, revealing the existence of older pictures hidden underneath supposedly ancient paintings. Chemical analyses are usually effective in determining the composition and age of materials. Metallic alloys had a different composition in the past, and though our knowledge of the subject is not complete, analysis can give us valuable circumstantial evidence. The situation is even more advantageous in ceramics, the clays and other elements of which have varied widely from region to region; the variations are generally quite well known. Therefore, if analysis reveals some element which did not exist at the place and time in question, we know that we are dealing with a forgery. Colours too have been mixed in different ways over the ages, and ancient texts often describe the methods and materials used, making it possible to verify the authenticity of "finds". Furthermore, some colours simply did not exist in the past. Prussian blue and zinc white have been used only since the eighteenth century, and cobalt blue and cadmium yellow only since the nineteenth century; their appearance on any object claimed to be earlier will give the game away at once.

A very recent method based on chemical tests, which will revolutionize the study of even the most remote period of prehistory is radiocarbon dating. This makes it possible to ascertain the date of any organic matter and will be ex-

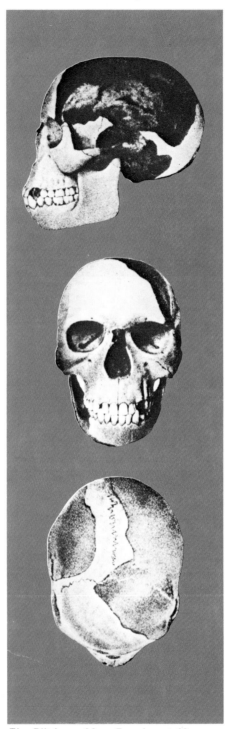

The Piltdown Man. For almost 40 years, scientists believed that Piltdown Man lived 1,000,000 years ago. However, in 1949 it was discovered that the jawbone and teeth came from a modern ape and had been made to look of great age. It was, in fact, a carefully planned hoax.

plained in the next chapter. Often, however, forgeries can be shown up by merely bringing to bear a wide general culture and a knowledge of the environment to which the work in question supposedly belongs. A famous case in point is that of the frescoes by Lothar Maskat, a German craftsman who was able to deceive the most renowned scholars into believing that his forgeries were Gothic works. The fraud was disclosed because of an environmental factor—the presence of turkeys in the paintings. These animals were imported to Europe centuries after the fictitious date of the frescoes.

Science uses all the means that have been described to detect fraud. Technical instruments, nevertheless, are only one aspect of the matter; the essential element is and will probably always be evaluation by the expert or art critic. A profound knowledge of the culture to which the work belongs, and of the author to whom it is attributed, and above all a sound aesthetic sense, are sure foundations for accurate judgements. The forger is, after all, a man of his age, using the tools available and applying the ideas current at the time. If stylistic analysis is applied thoroughly, and with the full employment of technical and cultural aids, a correct solution is almost certain.

Famous frauds

In the past things were different, for there were neither the scientific aids nor the daunting quantities of knowledge we now possess. Even now, many amateur collectors fail to have works they acquire examined by experts, thus inviting fraud. Also, many critics, having made a judgement, are reluctant to admit their mistakes when new facts emerge. These human factors continue to make frauds possible.

In some instances the forgery is relatively crude, and the delay in recognizing it is due to either the absence of experts or the superficiality of their examination. This occurred in the case of some earthenware with traces of writing on it, unearthed in 1924 at Glozel, near Vichy. At the time, it was claimed that they indicated the place of origin of the Western alphabet, going as far back as the Neolithic period! In fact, the forgery was the clever work of a peasant to whom an unscrupulous doctor had given the models—in other words it was a very unsophisticated piece of work despite the fact that circumstances endowed it with an ill-deserved fame.

On the same level are the imitations of Etruscan vases which can be found for sale at the big archaeological sites in Italy and Greece, which almost always provide the opportunity to set up a production centre. Usually the vendors are craft-shops, run as family concerns, that make a moderate profit by selling their products to foreigners as avowed imitations. Too bad if the customers do not recognize them as such and pay ridiculously high sums for them. At Grottaglie, near Taranto, for example, there are workshops of specialized potters who manufacture vases of "Greek style", often decorated with great care, but without any pretence to originality. Their light weight, the hollow sound they make when tapped, and the free mixing of patterns belonging to different styles clearly show, even to the most modest connoisseur, that they are not original ancient works.

Such workshops operate in the open and are entirely legitimate; the law does not forbid imitation—only fraud. The case is quite different when there is an intention to

This copy of a painted, terracotta warrior from the Metropolitan Museum in New York demonstrates how effective a good copy can be.

Left: a copy of the Kouros of the Glyptotek, Ny Carlsberg (Copenhagen)

Right: Diana the Huntress. (St Louis Museum, St Louis)

deceive. The Boston "throne", with marble reliefs, believed to be of the fifth century B.C., is just such a case. And the colossal "Etruscan" warriors made of terracotta, which were for many years on show at the Metropolitan Museum in New York, have only recently been recognized as forgeries. The same is true of the Kouros of the Glyptotek, Ny Carlsberg of Copenhagen, and of the Diana in the St Louis Museum —the work of Alceo Dossena, the prince of art forgers. At the beginning of the twentieth century

Dossena was making works that were only later found to be imitations—and even then experts were not always certain!

It has been justly said that the art of the forgers follows the fashion. The "Saitapharnes tiara", which was mentioned earlier, appeared at a time when there had been sensational discoveries of ancient jewellery; and fake Etruscan remains appeared in response to the fashion for Etruscan art. The list of frauds is endless, but only very few of them are in any way skilful. The work of forgers is popular mainly with the humbler collectors, who very seldom acquire objects of value and are reluctant to allow outside examination of an object they believe themselves to have obtained illicitly.

Illicit trade

Once forgeries have been made, the problem of how to sell them arises. And there is the same problem when it comes to disposing of authentic works of art which have been illicitly excavated by "tomb pirates". These excavations continue to flourish, in spite of the laws which forbid them, because they are so profitable. A partial solution was found in Sicily, where the "tomb pirates" were recruited as regular workers; but elsewhere the difficulty remains. Trade in both forgeries and illicitly acquired authentic works is much the same and the following remarks apply to both.

Illicit excavations and trading in archaeological material flourish in the countries that are still rich in buried treasures, such as Italy, Greece, Egypt and in the Near East. Neither the authorities in charge of protecting art treasures nor the police are able to keep every site under constant supervision, so theft is almost impossible to prevent. In addition the law varies from country to country. Some countries virtually favour the criminal wishing to sell antiquities of dubious ownership. Switzerland allows free trade in antiquities, and therefore Basle has become a centre where goods from Sicily, the south of Italy and Etruria are bought and sold. This trade is carried out mainly by middlemen and receivers, who often give the "tomb pirates" only a very small percentage of the profit.

Moving the sort of objects we have been discussing from one country to another is a form of smuggling, and as such it has the characteristics common to all forms of this practice. False bottoms in cars, crammed suitcases carried by people who are apparently beyond suspicion, and so on. Greek vases were once clandestinely exported, placed in chocolate egg boxes and sent abroad freely at Easter-time. Some archaeological objects are of great value but small in size, and therefore they are very easy to hide.

Laws and the archaeological conscience

The laws of countries rich in archaeological remains are naturally framed to make sure that finds are not exported: hence the flourishing of illicit trade. The fundamental point laid down by such laws is that the State owns the subsoil and everything in it, although there is usually a right of indemnity to the owners of

A famous forgery — the Saitapharnes tiara. (Louvre Museum, Paris)

ground where archaeological remains are buried. The same attitude underlies the right reserved by the State to control the use of such ground, forbidding building or other alterations, and where necessary appropriating the ground for further investigation. The prohibition of archaeological exports with a few rare and properly authorized exceptions, is the natural complement to this policy.

It is clear from this that the legislation of those countries directly involved shows an adequate awareness of the archaeological heritage and the problems arising from it. Unfortunately laws are not perfect and governments are in practice slow to intervene. Furthermore, the punishments laid down in legislation are usually too lenient, going no further than confiscation of objects of illicit origin or the imposition of small fines which do not in the least deter people used to handling large sums of money. At the most (and then only in a few cases) short terms of imprisonment may be imposed, and even these are often easily avoidable by putting up bail and/or securing an amnesty.

This state of affairs produces harmful results. Anyone who has, in his official capacity, brought an action against an unlawful possessor of illicit archaeological material, knows by experience that in the end no punishment will be meted out. In spite of expert witnesses who know the historical, cultural and commercial value of the objects illicitly held, the defending counsel usually manages to demonstrate that his client has acted in good faith, that he was unaware of the archaeological nature of the material, that he never intended to steal it, and so on. As we have seen, even if the guilty are sentenced, they will not necessarily go to prison, or at any rate not for long. Given the rich rewards of their activities, they will doubtless be glad to get off so easily, and more often than not will try their luck again, illicitly excavating or buying stolen archaeological goods.

Obviously it is necessary not only to tighten the law, but also to promote an archaeological conscience in order to stop such plundering. If we think back to Cicero's denunciation of Varro as a plunderer of works of art, if we remember Constantine's law prohibiting the removal of stones from urban buildings, we can see that such awareness was already present in the Classical world. This awareness seems to have disappeared altogether by medieval times. With the Renaissance and the Age of the Enlightenment, however, we find a steadily increasing consciousness of the value and significance of the ancient heritage.

Progress has continued ever since in this respect, as has been shown by the international conventions and exhibitions that link various countries. Enlightened collectors no longer keep works of art for their exclusive private pleasure but are happy to lend such works for public exhibition, often organized on an international basis and moved from city to city and even country to country. Reciprocal agreements ensure that the public in the countries concerned will benefit from exchanges. The successes that such initiatives have met with lately include the display of the Tutankhamun treasures in Paris, London and other cities following agreements between the countries concerned and Egypt; the Etruscan art exhibition in Vienna and in Stockholm promoted by Italy in collaboration with Austria and Sweden; the exhibition of Roman

A decorated obelisk at Karnak in Egypt.

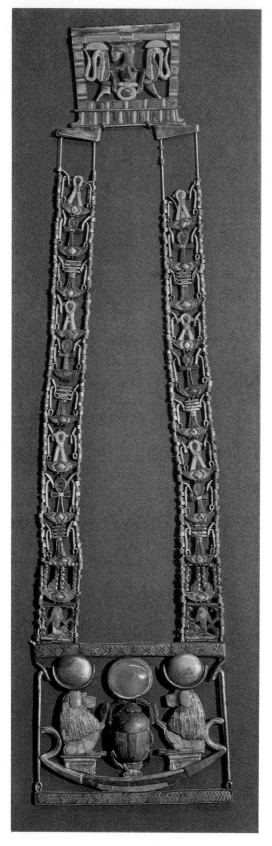

Three Egyptian treasures. Left: the breastplate of Sesostris II one of the rulers of Egypt during the Second Golden Age (2133–1625 B.C.). Above: a golden double casket from the tomb of Tutankhamun. Opposite: the back panel from Tutankhamun's throne showing the boy king being anointed with oil by his wife Ankhesnamun.

Tutankhamun's treasure was discovered by Howard Carter in 1922. When he entered the musty tomb his eyes gradually grew accustomed to the light. Details of the room slowly emerged, strange animals, statues and gold — everywhere the glint of gold. When asked if he could see anything, he replied, "Yes, wonderful things."

Because of the intense heat of the Egyptian summer, work could only be carried out during the cooler winter season. It took ten "seasons" to excavate the tomb completely and today all the treasures which were discovered are on display in Cairo Museum. Carter's relationship with the Egyptian Government deteriorated as the work progressed, and when work ended Carter and his colleagues received no reward whatsoever for their labours.

Two aspects of Thebes. Thebes is on the east bank of the Nile, and was associated with the god Amun. During the reign of the Pharaoh Mentuhotep (2065–2015 B.C.) it became capital and reached its height of importance during the 18th dynasty (1580–1314 B.C.) It began to decline after the Assyrian invasion of 664 B.C. and was finally destroyed during the reign of the Emperor Augustus. The two temples shown here testify to its grandeur.

art in Rumania; and the exhibition of ancient Chinese artefacts in London.

Even more impressive international initiatives are those that aim to establish procedures that will secure world-wide acceptance. The 1954 convention at The Hague established precise rules for the protection of works of art in the event of wars. A European project is also under discussion, aimed at the protection of archaeological heritage. It was proposed in 1964 to the European Council, and represents a first attempt to secure uniformity of legislation in artistic matters, which at present are still covered by very different legal principles, organizations, regulations, and even monetary and other penal sanctions.

UNESCO is a particularly effective institution for the protection of art treasures. For some years this organization of international scope and outlook has—thanks to the large sums of money at its disposal and to the huge number of experts it can call on—undertaken to rescue threatened archaeological and artistic treasures, no matter where they may be. Particularly wide publicity was given to the UNESCO campaign for the protection of the temples of Abu Simbel and other sites in Egypt, threatened with submersion by the waters of the great new dam on the Nile.

Initiatives and offers of collaboration were put forward in this instance purely in the interests of science, often by countries not entirely friendly to Egypt (or each other) on a political level. This demonstrates how far we have progressed since the time when archaeology was the exclusive property of a few experts and was practised within limits imposed by cultural, social and political barriers. In the activities of UNESCO there were signs of a new awareness on the part of large social classes. Archaeology assumes an almost symbolic function, and through it we may yet glimpse the tremendous possible benefits of co-operation between nations.

CHAPTER 8

BETWEEN PAST
AND PRESENT

So far we have looked at the fundamentals of archaeology. However the subject is not a static one, indeed at the moment it is going through a rapid evolution that will certainly transform it in the future. This last chapter is devoted to the beginnings of this transformation and to the aims and methods involved.

Because archaeology is affected by problems which also affect society in general, it must be placed within the context of society. This social dimension of archaeology is a significant characteristic of our time. In fact, the frontiers of archaeology are widening, and nowadays it is extremely difficult to be purely an archaeologist. The convergence of humanism and science, noted at the beginning of this book will become apparent again here.

A constantly changing science

Until relatively recent times, "archaeologist" was synonymous with "Classical scholar"; that is to say, one who has studied the history and culture of the Graeco-Roman world. But the discoveries of the last century or so have revealed the existence of dozens of civilizations and have led to a vast horizontal expansion of the archaeologist's field of study. More recent still are the archaeological developments on the vertical dimension; on the one hand the opening up of the immense subject of prehistory, and on the other the application of archaeological methods to the Middle Ages and even the Renaissance. Arguably the stratigraphy of a church is as important as that of an ancient monument, and the recognition and location of Christian ruins is now regarded as being as meaningful and important as the excavation of Greek and Roman cities.

These new developments mean that archaeologists must maintain more direct and continuous contacts with other sciences. For example linguistics, ethnology and folklore are now recognized as providing vital information and insights now considered essential to the archaeologist.

Thus there is an apparent paradox between the ever-widening horizons of archaeology and the tendency towards delimitation and specialization. The archaeologist must indeed be familiar with the problems and techniques of digging, but he must be no less well acquainted with the growing volume of historical, stylistic, technological and other data which have a bearing on his fieldwork. This explains the efflorescence of specialized schools of archaeology as well as the connections between the many different branches of research.

A gold embossed funeral mask from the Valley of the Cauca in Columbia. (Staatliche Museen Preussischer Kulturbesitz, Berlin)

111

Early cave carvings from Valcamonica. Above: a pair of oxen pulling a plough. Opposite above: deer and other animals grazing; below: a hunting scene.

Such cave carvings can be identified before the cave is entered by using special cameras.

Technical instruments

Modern techniques have made an enormous contribution to the transformation of archaeology; we have already remarked on the convergence of science and humanism, and we have also seen something of the specific techniques used to locate and evaluate archaeological finds. The complex of technical contributions to archaeological research comes under the heading of "sciences subsidiary to archaeology"; and this is proper in that it indicates the ultimate subordination of technique to judgement. Having dealt with the methods, we shall now concentrate on the instruments.

In photography, the most im-portant instrument is the camera whose eye can capture what lies underground so that digging is not needed. It is a instrument similar to that used in geological or hydro-logical drilling to identify mineral deposits and water strata. It is a very thin metallic tube into which a tiny camera with an electric flash has been inserted. The tube drills into the ground, penetrates any cavity and photographs its contents.

A highly specialized type of photo-graphic drill is the Nistri periscope (so called after its inventor), which consists of an optical apparatus similar to that of a submarine periscope, and a camera placed on the outside, near the eye-piece. This camera can be operated as and when

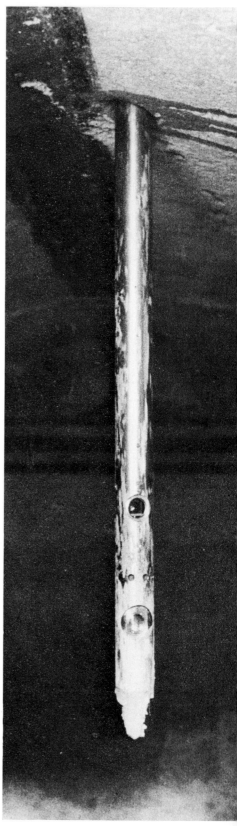

Above: using a periscope during an excavation. Right: a periscope probes the interior of an Etruscan tomb.

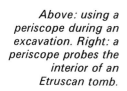

it is needed, so that little film is wasted. This system has been widely used by the Lerici foundation for the Tarquinian tombs, of which there are thousands, only a few bearing paintings on their walls. The preliminary photographs enabled the excavations to be carried out with maximum efficiency.

Besides the photographic drill, there is the so-called "carrot", which is used to draw samples of earth. It too derives from geological investigation, and consists of a metal tube which penetrates the earth a few metres deep, extracting a small

sample of soil without upsetting the stratification. The stratigraphy of numerous archaeological sites has been worked out in this way, samples taken in various parts of the excavation zone obviating the necessity for many laborious digs.

The motor pump, used in mines and building works to remove underground water, is often employed as a necessary preliminary to excavation. The most up-to-date motor-pump system is the one used by site workers at Sybaris an ancient Greek settlement on the Gulf of Taranto, in Italy. A set of metal tubes has been driven deep into the ground and linked on the surface by a collecting drum, through which big suction pumps suck up the water from below. In this way an excavation of such exceptional importance as the one at Sybaris, once impossible because of the presence of water-bearing strata, has become a reality.

The electromagnetic analysis of the ground, the importance of which was stressed when describing prospecting, is done mainly with an instrument called a "proton magnetometer". It registers with great

Wall paintings from the Giglioli Tomb at Tarquinia one of the centres of Etruscan civilization.

The excavation of the Greek settlement of Sybaris on the Gulf of Taranto in Italy. The city was founded in 720 B.C. by colonists from Achaea and Troezen. A large population was established and lived luxuriously, supported by produce from a very fertile soil. Sybaris became the chief entrepôt of trade between Greeks and Etruscans. The city was destroyed by the Crotons in 510 B.C., but the name still survives today in the word sybarite *which has come to mean luxury loving. Excavation here was particularly difficult because of the water-bearing soil structure, but this has now been overcome by using a sophisticated motor-pump system.*

sensitivity the variations of intensity in the magnetic field of the ground, pinpointing buried objects. It is true that magnetic anomalies are more difficult to recognize the deeper their origin, but the results obtained at Sybaris, where a wall has been located three metres below the ground, in England, where numerous remains have been revealed beneath Roman installations, and even at the bottom of the Dardanelles, where wrecks have been found hundreds of metres down, show just how successful the magnetometer can be used.

Instruments even more modern than the proton magnetometer, but based on the same principle, are the rubidium magnetometer and the caesium magnetometer. They have been used in southern Italy (at Sybaris and Metapont) and they have given precise and quick results, reducing the sensitivity to external agents. The use of these instruments is conditioned by the nature of the ground, the preliminary information available about the site, the distances involved and facilities for transporting the instruments, which is often extremely expensive. Such instruments have increased the efficiency of excavations but may have spoiled some of the romance attached to archaeology.

Methods of dating

A fundamental problem of archaeological research—in a sense the biggest problem—is dating the objects unearthed. In this field too, modern techniques have achieved exceptional results. Of all methods, currently the most impressive and widely applicable is the use of radio-carbon, without a doubt the most revolutionary discovery that has ever been made as far as the establishment of the chronology of the prehistoric and ancient world is concerned.

The fact on which radio-carbon dating is based is that every organic material contains a minute quantity of radio-active carbon (in technical terms C14), as well as ordinary non-radioactive carbon (C12). From the moment when the organic matter ceases to live, the radioactive carbon gradually decays; the rate of decay is constant and can therefore be used as a measure of time, usually expressed in terms of a half-life of the radioactive carbon of 5,600 years. It is evident that by measuring the quantity of remaining radio-carbon in organic matter it is possible to work out its age. Should that matter be trapped in a stratum of earth containing the remains of a settlement, the archaeologist can date the settlement without difficulty.

The great sensation caused by the discovery of radio-carbon dating (based on the chemical observations of Dr W. F. Libby of Chicago) is therefore entirely justified. Some limitations became clear as the method was applied, but they do not diminish its importance or validity; they merely indicate the possibility of errors and fluctuations in accuracy. First of all, the researchers who perfected the method realized that the dates supplied could vary between plus or minus 320 years and plus or minus 115 years: differences of no great importance in the prehistoric context, but great enough to deprive the method of most of its value when applied to historic times. Furthermore, samples of the same organic material, taken from the same place and in the same conditions, have been examined in different but equally reliable laboratories and have given different results. The same thing has happened within a single laboratory. For example, the laboratory of Gif-sur-Yvette has dated some wooden samples partly to 2250 B.C. $\pm$ 150 and partly to 1850 B.C. $\pm$ 150, although they originated from the same building. In fact a few experts question whether the radioactivity accumulated through the centuries at a constant rate or subject to some variations. A further difficulty is that of transferring the material to the laboratories while making sure that it remains entirely unchanged and unaffected by outside factors.

Another interesting method of establishing dates is dendrochronology, founded on the observations of the botanists who can tell the age of a tree from the horizontal section of its trunk, and in particular from the concentric rings, each representing one year in the life of the tree. This kind of analysis is of course limited to zones where timber was extensively used from ancient times and has remained in good condition; and it can only very rarely be used for a period of more than two or three millennia, and is therefore not available for the study of prehistoric ages.

Very complex, and therefore of limited use for the time being, is the method of analysis based on measurement of the magnetic field of ceramics. The same may be said of "thermoluminescence" applied to ceramics. The analysis of marshlands is also of interest, since sedimentation is closely linked to environmental conditions. The chemical spectographic analysis of metals can establish the nature of the "patina" resulting from their long residence underground. Finally, examinations of fossilized buried bones are also informative. They are based on the principle that bones slowly absorb fluorite from the ground in which they are buried, so that it is possible to work out a relative chronology from the percentage of fluorite absorbed.

The analysis of bones is linked with a very important kind of investigation developed by Russian scholars—that used to reconstruct the bodies of ancient men by examining their bones. This method is described by the Russian archaeologist A. Mongait: "It was in the USSR in particular that the system of reconstructing the faces of fossilised men by studying their skulls was perfected. This was a problem which scientists tried to solve for a long time. Various reconstructions were tried, but they were all diagrammatic and represented not so much prehistoric man as the idea of him that had formed in the scholar's mind. Eventually the archaeologist and anthropologist

M. Gherasimov demonstrated—accompanying his arguments with decisive proofs—that the soft tissues on the face were related to those of the skull bones, and on this basis he worked out principles by which the features could be reconstructed with absolute accuracy. The Gherasimov method has been checked more than once on human beings. This method has given us portraits of Pithecanthropi, of Sinanthropi, of Neanderthal men, of men of the Bronze Age, of the Scythians, and of historical figures such as Yaroslav the Great, Andrey Bogolyubsky and Tamerlane."

Another method of great interest developed by Russian archaeologists is the analysis of manufactured objects on the basis of wear and tear. This method is not so much concerned with dates as with the function of the objects, which traces of wear and tear in particular parts help to define. There are, in addition,

methods of only local application, for example the analysis of stratified clays which are the remains of the Ice Ages on the Baltic coast.

Archaeology in society

The instruments and techniques so far illustrated are not only useful for the interpretation of archaeological material; they also bring about an enrichment of the material itself, and of the material heritage of the country to which it belongs. This heritage also contributes in a relevant way to the economy as a tourist attraction. There are material as well as spiritual advantages in enhancing the landscape, in resurrecting ancient objects, cities, temples, villas; in short, in transforming a past which may be completely unknown, or alive only in literary sources, and presenting it in its archaeological context, as a direct testimony of a life buried for

The remains of the Minoan palace at Mallia in Crete. The royal burial ground close to Mallia has yielded many objects of great value including a ceremonial sword similar in design to those used in Ur.

119

The Great Sphinx was built as a monument to the Pharaoh Chephren, and portrays him as a great lion. Its early significance was forgotten in later centuries and the Egyptians came to worship it as a sun god. The sphinx measures 73 metres (240 feet) in length and 20 metres (66 feet) in height. Its face was mutilated in medieval times by Moslims, but even so it is still one of the most awe-inspiring sights in the world. An open temple was discovered between the front paws in 1816.

Below: Delphi, one of the centres of the cult of Apollo. Archaeologists have found Mycenaean idols which suggest that Gaea, Goddess of the Earth, was worshipped here, before Apollo became master of the sanctuary. In 376 B.C. the temple was destroyed by an earthquake, but it was rebuilt in the following years.

Above: The Temple of Amenophis III at Luxor. The magnificent colonnaded court and the great hall of columns are typical of the magnificence of everything the pleasure-loving Amenophis built. The temple was altered by later kings, and in Christian times it was turned into a church. Today it still has religious significance to Moslems.

Opposite: the scale of Amenophis III's magnificence is shown in this statue — one of the Colossi of Memnon at Thebes. The statue is 15 metres (50 feet) high and carved from one piece of sandstone carried from a quarry, almost 720 kilometres (450 miles) away.

centuries or millenniums.

Archaeological sites and relics of ancient civilizations are now a major tourist attraction. Different types of remains draw different types of tourists. Rome has long been a centre for all pious Catholics and Classical enthusiasts. Italy and France are the lands of pilgrimage for art lovers, and the Roman remains, historic buildings and traditions of Britain draw large numbers of transatlantic visitors. The expansion of air travel has put countries such as Tunisia, Egypt, the Lebanon, India, Mexico and Peru (all of which are rich in archaeological remains) within reach of tourists. Television programmes have lit the spark of enthusiasm for history in many people. It is to be hoped that countries endowed with archaeological resources will preserve and enrich them, so that this interest may be fostered and help to create an educated society which will care about its archaeological heritage.

The answer

The first chapter of this book posed the question "What is Archaeology?" Subsequent chapters tried to throw some light on a subject which is, all too often, shrouded in mystery. We have looked at the way in which archaeologists are trained, the methods used to excavate a site, the necessity for the archaeologists to publish the results of their work and the ways in which modern science is assisting the archaeologist in his work.

The old idea of archaeologists being inspired by the lure of treasure is no longer accurate. To the professional archaeologist every discovery, large or small, is equally satisfying in that it adds something to our store of knowledge of our history. The object of archaeology

today is not to dig for artefacts which will be proudly displayed in museums, but to find out how our ancestors lived and worked. Admittedly, the sensational finds which are featured in the newspapers bring archaeology into the public eye, but these are not important. What is important is that the archaeologists take advantage of the opportunities given to them today, but do so bearing in mind the duty they have to the public at large.

When he was asked "What in fact is Archaeology?", Sir Mortimer Wheeler once replied:

I do not myself really know. Theses have been written to demonstrate that it is this or that or not the other thing. . . . I constantly find it necessary to remind the student and indeed myself that the life of the past and the present are diverse but indivisible, that archaeology, in so far as it is a science, is a science which must be extended into the living and must indeed itself be lived in if it is to partake of a proper vitality.

Year after year, individual after individual, learned society after learned society, we are prosaically revealing and cataloguing our discoveries. Too often we dig up mere things, forgetful that our proper aim is to dig up people.

ACKNOWLEDGEMENTS

Balestrini: p. 40. Basle Natural History and Folk Museum: 32. Benedetti: 36, 39, 62–63, 77, 83, 86–87, 115. Bevilacqua: 106 (both), 107. Berlin Folk Museum: 110, 125. Brasa: 94. British Museum: 18, 33, 91. Carlsberg Gallery, Copenhagen: 102 (left). Central Italian Art Restoration Institute: 64, 72 (both), 73 (both). Dulevant: 23 (above). Editions Gallimard: 6, 8–9, 10, 17 (both), 19, 24–25, 29, 41 (both), 59, 60 (above and below), 74, 75 (above), 76, 120. La Bardo: 44. Lerici Foundation: 45, 46–47, 67, 114. Mairani: 11, 13, 26–27, 58, 85, 92–93, 119. Metropolitan Museum of Art: 101. Monaco Folk Museum: 124. Mondi: 68, 78. Moscati: 12, 14 (both), 15, 16, 30–31, 34, 53, 65, 75 (below). Museum of Etruscan Art, Cortona: 97. Nimatallah: 14 (above), 23, 43, 49. Pasagno Gallery: 80 (below). Passoti: 112–113. Poldi Pezzoli: 80. Reitz: 2, 20, 21, 23 (above), 35, 55, 56, 61 (both), 66, 84, 90, 105, 122. Rizzoli: 33 (above), 51, 70. St Louis Museum: 102 (right). Solomon R. Guggenheim Museum, New York: 81 (both). Superintendent of Antiquities, Basilicata: 69 (both). Superintendent of Antiquities at Calabria: 117. Superintendent of Antiquities at Salerno: 79. Superintendent of Antiquities at Naples: 52, 71 (both). Titus: 16 (below).

The quotation on pages 40–42 is from *Digging Up The Past* by Leonard Woolley and is included by permission of Ernest Benn, London.
The quotations on pages 52–53 and 124 are from *Archaeology From The Earth* by Sir Mortimer Wheeler and are included by permission of The Clarendon Press, Oxford.

FURTHER READING

Alexander, John. *Directing of Archaeological Expeditions*. New York: Humanities Press, 1970; London: J. Baker, 1970.

Baldwin, Gordon C. *Race Against Time: Story of Salvage*. New York: Putnam's Sons, 1966.

Braidwood, Robert J. *Archaeologists and What They Do*. New York: Franklin Watts, 1960.

Brennan, Louis A. *Beginner's Guide to Archaeology*. New York: Dell, 1974.

Ceram, C. W. (ed.). *The World of Archaeology: Archaeologists Tell Their Own Story*. London: Thames and Hudson, 1966; New York: Knopf, 1966.

Charles-Picard, Gilbert (ed.). *Larousse Encyclopedia of Archaeology*. New York: Putnam's Sons, 1972.

Cousteau, Jaques-Yves. *Diving for Sunken Treasure*. London: Cassell, 1971; New York: Doubleday, 1972.

Cotterell, Leonard. *The Lion Gate*. London: Evans Bros., 1966.

— *Lost Civilizations*. Glasgow: William Collins, 1974; New York: Franklin Watts, 1974.

Dietz, James (ed.). *Man's Imprint From the Past: Readings in the Methods of Archaeology*. Boston: Little Brown, 1971.

Harrison, Michael. *London Beneath the Pavement*. London: Peter Davies, 1961.

Irwin, Constance. *Fair Gods and Stone Faces*. New York: Saint Martin's Press, 1963; London: W. H. Allen, 1964.

Kenyon, Kathleen. *Archaeology in the Holy Land*. London: Ernest Benn, 1965; New York: Praeger Press, 1970.

McKee, Alexander. *History Under the Sea*. London: Hutchinson, 1968.

Moffat, Robert K. *Going on a Dig: A Guide to Archaeological Field Work*. New York: Hawthorn, 1975.

Morrison, Alexander (ed.). *Collins Concise Encyclopedia of Archaeology*. Glasgow: William Collins, 1968.

Pearson, John. *Arena: The Story of the Colosseum*. London: Thames and Hudson, 1973; New York: McGraw-Hill, 1973.

Watts, Edith W. *Archaeology: Exploring the Past*. New York: Metropolitan Museum of Art, 1965.

INDEX

Italic page numbers refer to illustrations